CONVERSATIONS
WITH
JESUS

CALVIN MILLER

D0061966

HARVEST HOUSE PUBLISHERS

EUGENE, OREGON

Calvin Miller: Published in association with the literary agency of WordServe Literary Group, Ltd., 10152 S. Knoll Circle, Highlands Ranch, CO 80130

The 2006 copyright date applies to the opening prayer in each devotion.

Cover photo © James P. Blair/Photodisk Green/Getty Images

Cover by Koechel Peterson & Associates, Inc., Minneapolis, Minnesota

CONVERSATIONS WITH JESUS
Copyright © 1998/2006 by Calvin Miller
Published by Harvest House Publishers
Eugene, Oregon 97402
www. harvesthousepublishers.com

Library of Congress Cataloging-in-Publication Data

Miller, Calvin.
  Conversations with Jesus / Calvin Miller.
    p. cm.
  ISBN-13: 978-0-7369-1752-0 (pbk.)
  ISBN-10: 0-7369-1752-7
  1. Jesus Christ—Biography—Devotional literature.   2. Devotional calendars.   I. Title.
  BT306.53.M55 2006
  232.9'01—dc22   2005017666

Printed in the United States of America

        06   07   08   09   10   11   12   13   14   / DP-MS /   10   9   8   7   6   5   4   3   2   1

*To Jesus
and to Barbara,
who often makes me
think of him.*

TO THE READER

I have often read through the life of Christ, asking myself what Jesus would like to say directly to me. His instructions came as I used a harmony of the Gospels to listen to the events of his life as they unfolded through his ministry. My pilgrimage lasted several years, and then in the course of a few months I recorded my experience in a 365-day format. This devotional guide became a kind of reckoning with him about the specifics of his will—a listening walk with the Master. The book you now hold chronicles the first third of my journey.

As is true of all that I have written, I have sought a lot of help in preparing this manuscript. Barbara's endless typing and editing have made this work possible. Once again I have relied on my great friend and counselor in prayer, Deron Spoo. To all who have worked to make this book a possibility, I am most grateful.

If you choose to walk with Christ during that same unfolding of his years, simply read these devotions day by day. After all, day by day is how he lived his life too. May I suggest that you note in the margin of this guide the specific things he may be saying to you that vary from what I felt him saying to me. You may even want to create your own daily journal of interaction with the Bible. I find that as I write in his presence, I remember longer the exact words of those instructions he means for me alone.

I realize the risk of putting words in the mouth of Christ that are not his. However, every time I sat to write, I strove to be sure that I did not have him say things that would contradict what is in the Bible. This was most important to me. Perhaps Thomas à Kempis, writing of Christ in the same way, has influenced me by way of precedent. Besides the Scriptures, no work has influenced me like his. I know I have not done it as well as he did, but I intended to borrow from his lofty example.

I do hope our mutual examination of the life and teachings of Christ will make us friends. As friends of Jesus, we ought to strengthen each other by virtue of our common worship and our concern for each other. Perhaps the real theme of this volume is "O come let us adore him...together."

Calvin Miller
Birmingham, Alabama

1

JESUS, I WANT TO START OVER

LUKE 3:1-2
Now in the fifteenth year of the reign of Tiberias Caesar, when
Pontius Pilate was governor of Judea, and Herod was tetrarch of
Galilee, and his brother Philip was tetrarch of the region of Ituraea
and Trachonitis, and Lysanias was tetrarch of Abilene, in the high
priesthood of Annas and Caiaphas, the word of God came to John,
the son of Zacharias, in the wilderness.

LORD,
I come to you today in a dead-end moment. I can't seem
to get started doing anything important. I want to. I
want to live for really important reasons. I want to start
over. I want to begin now.

I am the Lord of beginnings and the Lord of beginners. Every dawn is
the perfect place for a new start. Each new day is the beginning of the rest
of your life. So where you were is no impediment to where you are going.

I began my own saving ministry in the fifteenth year of Tiberias.

Luke begins his account of my life with what may seem to you histori-
cal tedium. The fifteenth year of Tiberias? Does Luke seem too interested
in who ruled what? The point is that my Father always acts in such a way
as to gild the ordinary moments of somebody's history. Remember that
every act of God occurred when someone was ruler of something.

But now my earthly history is done.

What about yours?

I want you to measure the importance of your life in how well you pass
on the love I have given you. I want you to see your years as important
because you have given them to me.

Still, I didn't come merely to challenge you to better yourself. I came
for all people—the millions throughout time whose mini-histories never
made the books. I came so all who live unremarkable lives and die in

unmarked graves would be able to say, "I believed in Jesus in my own particular corner of history, and like him, I am alive forevermore." The life I came to give you is yours to use. Live the days for me. If you do not, it will be as though I never came at all.

So enjoy your time on earth. But be wise. Your time will be brief. As you walk your hurried decades, I will make your life rich with my presence. Arise daily to celebrate my purpose for you, and you will be born anew each sunrise. Sip the joy of my everlasting love, but do it day by day.

LORD JESUS,
I'm up. I'm aware.
I'm claiming the day.
Today is the perfect place to begin the rest of my life.
In this brief, hurried day I will make you
sovereign over every second. I will call you Lord of every moment,
Master of the 24/7, owner of my watch, keeper of my calendar.

I've called you Lord of my brief history.
Come wrap me in your saving mystery.
Amen.

2

ODD PEOPLE

MATTHEW 3:3-5
"For this is the one referred to by Isaiah the prophet, saying, 'The voice of one crying in the wilderness, "Make ready the way of the Lord, Make His paths straight!"'" Now John himself had a garment of camel's hair, and a leather belt about his waist; and his food was locusts and wild honey. Then Jerusalem was going out to him, and all Judea, and all the district around the Jordan.

LORD,
odd people are hard to love, and I am surrounded by them. They are all spines and thorns. Touch them, and sooner or later they sting you. Can you please change the world so I will like it more?

Change the world for your sake? No, I shall change you for the sake of the world. Change all the people you consider odd? No, I shall change you so you can learn the art of loving people different from yourself.

I have a cousin whom the world saw as odd. He avoided the cities and survived by eating grasshoppers and field honey. His name: John the Baptist. He came as the emcee of a new age. He came when time was turning the AD corner. I was about to step into the human story. Mere political empires would soon be rendered temporary by the eternal importance of my kingdom. In me the Almighty was on earth like a king awaiting a fanfare.

And who was to play this fanfare?

This very odd man named John. John was perfect for the job. He was odd but real. He knew how to keep a low profile in the presence of dignity. He had learned how to step down from the theater of human applause to treasure the applause of God.

Remember this: The most dedicated sometimes seem odd. If you do not appear odd sometime in your life, you will likely be so hung up on being approved by everybody, you will be of no real use to anybody.

John Bar Zacharias was his whole name. He rarely ever used it. He wasn't ashamed of it. He just wasn't stuck on his own identity. He didn't want to be a personality. He was content to be a voice crying in the wilderness. He was God's odd man, heaven's hermit, a herald in camel's hair.

Like John, seek simplicity in your life, and you will be used of God. Learn to wear the camel's hair of spiritual inwardness. Embrace me in the needy wilderness of your own devotion. It could be that in time people will see you as odd. But when you love me as you should, your need for a better reputation will lose much of its power over you.

Practice John's submission. If you point to yourself and say, "Here I am!" the world will soon ignore you. But if you point to me and say, "There is Jesus, the Lamb of God!" the world will stand in the joyous whirlwind of your pronouncement. Have courage! Go past the narrow gates of your own small self-importance, and you will find the immensity of God.

LORD JESUS,
I am in need of love—your love!
I am irregular. I am needy. I am odd.

Teach me to own my odd identity
and serve you as I am in honesty.
Amen.

3

KNOCK DOWN THE BARRIERS; I'M ON MY WAY TO YOU

LUKE 3:5-6
Every ravine shall be filled up, And every mountain and hill shall be brought low; And the crooked shall become straight, And the rough roads smooth; And all flesh shall see the salvation of God.

LORD,
I'm on the way, and my need for you has set me on a run to you. Is there anything between us? Is the road I must travel to be in your presence completely level?

Yes, yes! Run to me. I am eager to embrace you with a confidence you seem to have lost. I've taken every barrier down. Come back to the center of my love. I've prepared your way—made it smooth like a highway laid in an open desert. I've hauled the mountains down. I've filled in all the ravines. I've taken all the curves out of the road ahead. Your vision is unobstructed!

The way back to me is clear. You will have no trouble finding me. I am standing in the open center of God's grace. My love has made the rough ways smooth for your return.

Let your journey home begin before the dawn. I am light; walk toward me. If you want to know your place in relation to the light, watch the birth of morning. The lesser stars will fade. The sky will soon yield its velvet blackness to the paling east.

I will be there—the one light that defies the coming sun. I have been steady through the dark night, for I am the Morning Star. I will linger long after the sun has forced its way into the morning.

I will be the light for your journey through life. Your way will be smooth and well lit. Go therefore! Tell all you meet, "God has prepared you a highway in the desert." No ravines! No curves! No mountains! Nothing bars the way. Point to me and say, "See, God is at the gates of your life. He is the light that pushes sunrise. Cast off your despair. Christ is at hand. Cleanse your hearts. Get ready for his presence. Look and see the salvation of God. Hope."

LORD JESUS,

I know that if I do not see your salvation,
it is because I have chosen to be blind.
But I am physician in this matter.
I will not live in willful darkness.
You have made the way level.
You have lit the journey with grace.

And on the level road I clearly see
your love is sunlight in resplendency.
Amen.

4

CHILDREN FROM STONES

MATTHEW 3:7-9

But when he saw many of the Pharisees and Sadducees coming for baptism, he said to them, "You brood of vipers, who warned you to flee from the wrath to come? Therefore bring forth fruit in keeping with repentance; and do not suppose that you can say to yourselves, 'We have Abraham for our father'; for I say to you, that God is able from these stones to raise up children to Abraham."

LORD,
I feel pretty good. About myself, I mean. I'm a member of a church, you know. I have been for a long time now. My grandparents took my parents to church, and my parents took me. That's how I got to be so religious. I am nearly a genetic Christian. I was "born" a church member. I'm a Christian by tradition.

Tradition can be wonderful, but it can also be like backing into the future. The Pharisees were so fascinated with what God had done, they found little interest in what he was about to do. Tradition is most healthy when it leads us to celebrate the great acts of God. Tradition is a moonlight swim through a balmy heritage. But beware of becoming entangled in the past. The future is where God is leading you.

Why are you so intrigued with your membership in a denomination? Could it be because tradition is safe? Celebrating what was is never as risky as walking into what could be. Old doctrines are as charming as they are settled. The past inspires great hymns and poems. It is error free. You can't mess up yesterday. Still, yesterday is an anchor in the past that can delay the voyages of your life. You must weigh anchor and sail the open sea ahead.

The Pharisees loved their traditions. They loved honoring Abraham. After all, he had been dead for 1700 years. It was John the Baptist's fiery new messianism that left them edgy. John wasn't someone you wrote hymns about. His demands were all for the moment. Consider John and face my demands for your life. Do not offer me your church certificates or tell me how great your heritage has been. I want one thing from you—your tomorrow.

John may have lacked tact but not honesty. He thundered against these keepers of yesterday, "You snakes! Get out of the way of the all-consuming fire of the new. The new is coming…the kingdom of God. Don't tell us you are Abraham's children. God can make from these desert stones such children." God has never been content to be praised just for what he used to do. He is Lord of the right now! He forbids all who claim to love him to sit in the center of his highway to the future and play with their heritage.

Never over-cherish your traditions. Do not over-prize your church membership. Cherish rather the God of tomorrow. Keep your eyes on the will-be. It's the surest way to avoid becoming a has-been.

LORD JESUS,
each day I would remember
which allegiances are prior and
which are not.
I want to live on that thin strip of time where
the past and future meet.
I want to examine the past only long enough
to thank you for the heritage that produced me.

Then I'll turn and follow you as one—
to claim that "yet" where life is lost or won.
Amen.

5

BAD PEOPLE
OF THE WORLD, UNITE

LUKE 3:10-14

And the multitudes were questioning him, saying, "Then what shall we do?" And he would answer and say to them, "Let the man who has two tunics share with him who has none; and let him who has food do likewise." And some tax-gatherers also came to be baptized, and they said to him, "Teacher, what shall we do?" And he said to them, "Collect no more than what you have been ordered to." And some soldiers were questioning him, saying, "And what about us, what shall we do?" And he said to them, "Do not take money from anyone by force, or accuse anyone falsely, and be content with your wages."

LORD,
I know I don't deserve your love. Am I good enough to be used? I feel bad about myself.

John the Baptist knew how valuable bad people could be. He attracted a lot of tax-gatherers to get the kingdom going. The religious leaders doubted that tax-gatherers were the best place to start the kingdom. They said to use these tax-gatherers was like trying to build a sacrificial world with tycoons. It seemed to the Pharisees that new religions should start with notable philanthropists or religious scholars. But John could see that tax-gatherers really were the best starting place. Most people generally agreed that tax-gatherers were pretty bad people, so they were less defensive about their morality. Tax-gatherers knew they cheated people. Everybody knew it. When your sins are this obvious, you don't really need to confess them. Other people will do it for you.

Beware of becoming such a celebrated religionist; you have trouble really seeing yourself as a sinner. You may have a hard time living openly in front of the church. Beware of "churchy" respectability; it can become a mask that keeps anyone from ever seeing you as a needy person.

Let your own need cause you to ask, "What do you do with people whose repentance seems a blight on being good?"

John baptized them and offered them a new beginning in God's kingdom.

When they were baptized, they left their brokenness beneath the Jordan. They watched with tears in their eyes as all of their self-sufficiency swirled away in the brown river water. Then what joy came! These happy new tax-gatherers felt great. They knew that across town there were Pharisees whose confessions were more literary. But no matter. It is good to know who you are—to live without pretense. Then you can wade out of the river a new person.

What would happen to you if you became this real? But how your critics view you makes you all the more ready for the Christ-life. The kingdom of God is born within you at exactly the place where your need for religious respectability is less important than the hunger to be clean. I tell you it's the bad people who really are the best symbols of transformation. It's the bad people who finally become real enough to be world changers.

LORD JESUS,
how long has it been since my sins were so obvious
I had to confess them?
I'm such a discreet sinner that I need to ask you to shine
the light of your grace fully on my need.
Teach me that tears are the distillation of utter honesty.
Help me cherish the confession of reformed tax-collectors.
I'm Pharisee enough already.

I'll know my penance real when I have cried
and given up my stiff religious pride.
Amen.

6

BAPTIZED BY FIRE

MATTHEW 3:11
As for me, I baptize you with water for repentance, but He who is coming after me is mightier than I, and I am not fit to remove His sandals; He will baptize you with the Holy Spirit and fire.

LORD,
I'm a Christian, but I have the blahs! Life is drab. Things just aren't all that exciting. I used to burn for God, but I confess the flame is gone. I used to be on fire, but lately there is no fire. All that once burned bright within me is covered with gray ash. What's the key to staying alive all through life?

No fire, you say! Have you made a god of your cold propriety? The real passions of the honest heart can never be hidden. You must feel a thing to know that it is real. You must feel something to know that you are real. The rage that shakes your frame, the love that warms your heart, the unhallowed fear that raises the hair on the nape of your neck...these passions tell you you're alive, and they tell you what matters to you.

The stronger you feel about anything, the more you know you are alive. There are those who will tell you that their religion is totally inward. If it is so inward it never surfaces, it is nonexistent. What you really feel, you cannot hide. What you really believe proclaims itself. All real faith is exhibitionist! It dances openly in the daylight.

Remember the disciples on the Day of Pentecost? Joy came in tongues of fire and rushing wind. A tempest of love had settled on the church. They spoke with tongues ecstatically and all at once. The mystery confounded them, and all those who saw were amazed that they heard in the languages that they had never learned.

"They are full of sweet wine," said their critics (Acts 2:13).

"Hardly," said Peter. "This is that which was spoken by the prophet Joel; And it shall come to pass in the last days, saith God, I will pour out of my Spirit upon all flesh: and your sons and your daughters shall prophesy, and your young men shall see visions, and your old men shall dream dreams" (Acts 2:16-17 KJV). Why this disruptive, delirious exhibitionism? God had visited them. How wonderful...fire! The light of the night, the warmth of winter!

Please hear John's own prophecy of me. "After me One is coming who is mightier than I, and I am not fit to stoop down and untie the thong of His sandals. I baptized you with water, but He will baptize you with the Holy Spirit" (Mark 1:7-8). How gloriously my Father chops into mundane living with exotic joy. Those who might have said they wanted something quiet were given something gloriously boisterous. Those who would have felt cozy with a dull and church-tamed mood found themselves afire.

It is a cold formality that says, "Please. I want a religious experience I can feel comfortable with. Let me worship God in my own inner way! I like tasting God one bite at a time, from my demitasse and doily. I keep my lovely Jehovah in a jar...a silver jar, of course."

Come with me and really live. All great faith is asbestos. It craves the open flame. Make such a flame your inner fire: Take me on my terms. Welcome those passions that are too large to hide beneath your timid propriety. Let your love declare itself. Be combustible. Joy is fire!

LORD JESUS,
forgive me for wanting to serve you
on my own terms.
Forgive me for making you a discussion
and forgetting that you would prefer to be a consuming fire.
Forgive me for wanting my faith to be so tidy and liturgical
that I keep my passions zipped in my prayer book.
Give me more than I think I want.
Help me to cherish an affection that others
think excessive.

Baptize me in the ardor of desire,
not water, Lord. I beg you for the fire.
Amen.

WHEAT GOOD, CHAFF BAD

MATTHEW 3:12
And His winnowing fork is in His hand, and He will thoroughly
clear His threshing floor; and He will gather His wheat into the
barn, but He will burn up the chaff with unquenchable fire.

LORD,
have I cared too much about things that are not eternal?
Loving the transient and ignoring the eternal is such a
snare—forgive me, Lord. I am a captive to the secular
advance. I've traded the miracles of God for the tricks of
the glitzy world. I am too much chaff, too little grain.

Chaff is both worthless and loved.

A grain of wheat is a remarkable thing. It is really a small plant in
embryo. It is impatient life willing to sleep only until the temperature and
water are just right. Give it a tiny drink and keep it warm, and its thin shell
will split. The plant will send its silky head toward sunlight and its silver
roots into the dark earth.

But chaff! It holds no embryo. You can water it forever. Nothing will
burst inside it. No life will come. Nor sprout shoot up. No roots go down.
Chaff is a dead thing that will not reproduce itself, ever. Here is my Father's
most insistent command: Cherish only that which can reproduce itself. Be
not like chaff.

Be like a grain of wheat, holding within yourself the promise of life.

It is not a hostile act that leads my Father to destroy the chaff. He does
not hate chaff. He is God. He knows no grudge, nor can he hate anything.
But chaff is worthless; it is in the way. It mires and threatens honest life. It
collects above the wheat to steal its sun. It soaks the moisture that might
cause real grain to live and grow. So God grieves the chaff. He grieves all
things dead if they are content to remain so.

Consider the lesson of the winnowing fork. The fork throws both grain and chaff into the wind. But only the grain has substance enough to settle back to the threshing floor. The chaff, of little substance, is caught by the wind and carried away.

Sadly, chaff is often possessed of such flighty arrogance, it supposes itself to be more than it is. The ungodly, said the psalmist, are like that chaff, which the wind drives away (Psalm 1:6). While presuming themselves to be people of real content, the ungodly prove at last there's nothing of substantial value in their lives.

God is looking for that good seed that produces fruit. Strive to be a person of substance—to contain the life principle. Strive to pass the test of the winnowing fork.

LORD JESUS,
when the winnowing comes and the Lord of the harvest
seeks those whose lives reproduced themselves,
help me to be numbered among those who cherish substance,
who glory in the principle of life.

Blow wind through me till I hear heaven laugh,
and treasure substance and despise the chaff.
Amen.

WHAT IS MY PLACE IN THE WORLD?

MATTHEW 3:13-15

Then Jesus arrived from Galilee at the Jordan coming to John, to be baptized by him. But John tried to prevent Him, saying, "I have need to be baptized by You and do You come to me?" But Jesus answering said to him, "Permit it at this time; for in this way it is fitting for us to fulfill all righteousness." Then he permitted Him.

LORD,
    I feel so separate and alone. I feel as if I have hardly any friends, and the few I do have seem distant and remote. I wonder if I require more loyalty from them than I give to them. I wonder if I want them to be at my beck and call, without feeling that I need to be at theirs. I feel a sense of being all alone in the world without any support. Have I come to grips with the idea that the kingdom is a community of the needy, and the best that the church has to give is the idea that the needy serve each other?

It is time you quit asking, "Why do I have so few friends?" and begin to ask, "What are the needs I might supply to my world, which so often seems to ignore me?"

John was baffled the day I asked him to baptize me. John's baptism symbolized the washing away of sin. I had never sinned, and John knew it. But I knew the definition of baptism would be growing. I knew that the church would someday define it as more than the mere washing away of sin. In time it would come to stand for identity with the people of God. So I said to John, "It is fitting!"

How true that was.

There was no finer way for me to endorse what John was teaching than to allow him to baptize me. By letting him baptize me I said clearly, "All that John has been teaching is right. I take my stand with John. See, I submit to him. John and I are both in this world pursuing one thing: the kingdom of God." All who saw that baptism knew that John and I were not each vying to start our own separate religions. We were one in the purpose of forming the new community of God. So we met in the river Jordan, the thin river that was always colored brown by the flux of desert silt. Yet when the sun fell full upon the Jordan that day, it was gold.

We met there within the heart of God. We threw our faces to the sky and praised the new order that was on the way. The kingdom of God was here and now! I fell full backward into the joy of the world's glorious new beginning. The water closed over me. The old was gone. And when I rose back through the eddies of the golden Jordan, the new order had been born.

This is the way of the river. Have you declared yourself as a member of the kingdom? Be baptized. The world is your agenda. Be baptized and leave all your little reasons to live beneath the water. Wade out of the water and cry, "What next, God?"

LORD JESUS,
here am I in utter need of your particularity.
You are my singular Lord.
If I was the only one who had needed it, you would have died for me.
If I was the only one who felt lonely, you would still walk with me.
Thank you for giving me a place of significance in your community.

I met you first with vows where water flowed.
We walk as friends one quiet, needy road.
Amen.

WHEN GOD SAYS, "YOU REALLY ARE A WONDERFUL HUMAN BEING!"

MATTHEW 3:16-17

And after being baptized, Jesus went up immediately from the water; and behold, the heavens were opened, and he saw the Spirit of God descending as a dove, and coming upon Him, and behold, a voice out of the heavens, saying, "This is My beloved Son, in whom I am well-pleased."

LORD,
I feel so unappreciated. My life is running short of compliments. I can't remember when anyone said, "Nice job" or "What an accomplishment!" I guess I just need to feel a little more appreciation than the world gives me.

I understand your need for affirmation. Compliments are simple yet helpful. They lift you from your own captivity to your poor self-image and set you free to achieve a better life.

After I was baptized, I heard the voice that ricocheted across the waters. But it was not the voice alone I treasured. Rather I treasured him whose voice I heard. God's voice affirmed my sonship. Since my chief delight was to bring pleasure to my Father, my joy burst forth at his compliment.

This *bath qol*, this loud voice, was the confession of God. "This is my Beloved! I am pleased with him." God felt for me what I felt for him. I lived to please him. I sought only to delight myself in his perfect pleasure.

Tell me, do you have a child? Well, no matter. Whether or not you *have* one, it is certainly true that you *are* one. Think of those times when you and your parents were welded into oneness. Was it not those times that your parents were so spontaneously proud of you that their pride erupted before some gathering of family or friends? How important it is to compliment your child. If there is no one to hear your compliment, your pride itself will shout your affirmation to the wind. If none applaud your child, the rocks themselves will cry out.

Such times of special affirmation can never be diminished. For on that day the voice called out, I realized it was my Father's oneness with me that was the fount of all my joy. I also realized that his affirmation and praise meant more to me than anyone else's ever could.

What is it that fuels your spirit and makes you hungry to please God? If you are truly my brother, honestly my sister, you must certainly care about what God thinks. And if you really care what God thinks, you will relish his compliment and be broken by his censure.

Someday, of course, his great compliment to you will be "Well done... you have been faithful over a few things, I am about to make you a ruler over many." Every life well lived is one that loves me and waits for that compliment. When that day comes and when at last you begin to thrill at the compliment of God, you will know the joy I felt that day at the Jordan River. Spend your entire soul and every waking moment of your life to purchase such a compliment. Desire it. It is the only compliment that matters.

LORD JESUS,
it is the plainness of your Father's announcement
that is so thrilling.
It is clear that heaven held no shame
in your incarnation.
Help me to be as forthright
in announcing that you are my Lord
as God was in announcing
you are his Beloved.

To please you is my one magnificent confession.
Your compliment, my most magnificent obsession.
Amen.

WHEN AND WHERE SHALL I BEGIN TO TAKE UP MY CROSS?

LUKE 3:23
And when He began His ministry, Jesus Himself was about thirty years of age.

LORD,
I'm all dressed up with nowhere to go. I want to serve you, but where is the gate of my beginning? Where do I start my service? Will it really matter if I don't?

From the vantage point of your walk with God, do you see mostly question marks? It was true for me, as well. In becoming a man, I gave up my use of many of the attributes of my godhood. One was explicit foreknowledge. I knew I was God's Son, and I knew I would die for human sin. But where to start? At what exact moments would I pass the certain points on the calendar?

I knew too that my life would not be long. And yet I also knew that my years would be the most significant to pass across the globe. There was but one question that occupied my days. Morning by morning I rose and asked, "What is it you have for me to do today, Father?" The future is born in the moment at hand.

There really are only two rules for you. First, number your days. This will make you a good steward of your years. Did not the psalmist say, "Teach us to number our days, that we may apply our hearts unto wisdom" (Psalm 90:12 KJV)?

The second rule is this: Your life is not your own. You gave it away when you claimed me as your Lord. Since your life belongs to me, your desire with each sunrise should be, "Lord, what do you want me to do today?" Such one-day-at-a-time love for me will fill your years with meaning.

Learn to see the various seasons of your life in two ways. First, do not grudge those waiting times when you are struggling to know what God wants with you and how you are to accomplish it. This part of my own life took thirty years. The second part of your life must consist in the faithful pursuit of what you know to be God's will. This second part of my life took only three years. Which part is most important? They share equally in the importance. My first thirty years were lived with that consistency that knew no sin. My final three years were also sinless, but they yielded to God's plan, which, once discovered, drove me to please my Father by completing all he asked.

Let us not talk of life's hardness but of its sweetness. For once I knew the obligation of the cross, I knew my union with my Father would be all-important.

Would you make your life sweet? You have only to obey all my Father asks.

Nothing that he asks will be easy. But it will be glorious. Glorious because the rigors of his requirements will cause you to need him. Then God will become for you not a luxury but a sweet necessity. Pray for such a necessity. Live in such a communion.

LORD JESUS,
it is not the number of years you have given me
but the calling
that will mark my life as significant.
Neither when I start nor when I finish
is as important
as how I completed what you gave me to do.

It's not enough to know our future days;
the current day alone elicits praise.
Amen.

ACCEPTING THE SLICE AND SAYING NO TO THE LOAF

MATTHEW 4:1-4
Then Jesus was led up by the Spirit into the wilderness to be
tempted by the devil. And after He had fasted forty days and forty
nights, He then became hungry. And the tempter came and said
to Him, "If you are the Son of God, command that these stones
become bread." But He answered and said, "It is written, 'Man shall
not live on bread alone, but on every word that proceeds out of the
mouth of God.'"

LORD,
 will I someday learn the art of saying no to myself? Will
I ever really learn to deny myself? I want to, but I also
want to indulge myself. My appetites too often master
my common sense. How shall I ever learn to say no to
second helpings of everything that's not good for me?

The power of the positive no is essential to your life of faith! I knew this
temptation in the desert, where Satan came to tempt me. Doesn't he always
come at such times? He knows those moments when our defenses are weak-
est. I well remember our meeting in the wilderness. I had just ended a 40-
day fast, and I was ravenous with hunger. The Tempter was lurking in the
shadows. Isn't he always? With a curl in his lip he simply asked, "Hungry?"

He knew I was. His question caused my eyes to fall on some rounded
stones. They looked as round and brown as the loaves of bread my mother
once baked in Nazareth. They needed only my command to become what
I really wanted them to be.

Oh, I was hungry!

As I studied the stones, I thought of all my power. I knew I could do it.
I could actually turn stones to bread. Then the voice of the Tempter came
once again from the shadows: "Why not?"

I did not yield. I understood that to use the power of God to indulge my appetites was set against all I would later teach about self-denial. If I had used even one tiny quantum of power to change those stones to bread, I might have next changed the dust to butter and the fallen leaves to jam.

Do you sense there is a downward progression in the licenses you grant yourself?

Appetites can tempt you to become totally self-serving. They can lure you to have *what* you want, *when* you want to have it. They can deceive you into believing that you no longer have to wait on anything. Finally you will become only the sum of all your cravings.

Are there stones in your life that are right now begging you to change them into what seems a sweet indulgence? Are you jealous because someone in the corporation was promoted above you? Are you toying with sexual infidelity? At every juncture, the Enemy is in the shadows saying to you, "Why not? And why not right now?" Beware! Your yielding at any point will only make Satan's work all the easier the next time. Drunkenness, gluttony, and infidelity, which seem gratifying at first, in the end bring only captivity. Addictions begin in the act of changing one little stone into one little loaf. Be careful. Do not yield. Deny yourself. Live free.

LORD JESUS,
my appetites tell others who I am.
Let them keep me informed as well.
It does no good to claim publicly that I belong to you
while I pursue my private lusts.

Help me to put my passions underneath
those promises committed to your keep.
Amen.

LORD, WHAT ABOUT MY FIFTEEN MINUTES OF FAME?

MATTHEW 4:5-6

Then the devil took Him into the holy city; and he had Him stand on the pinnacle of the temple, and said to Him, "If You are the Son of God throw Yourself down; for it is written, 'He will give His angels charge concerning You'; and 'On their hands they will bear You up, Lest You strike Your foot against a stone.'" Jesus said to him, "On the other hand, it is written, 'You shall not put the Lord your God to the test.'"

LORD, it seems I achieve so little. Athletes and movie stars dominate the culture. They make millions while I work hard for little pay and no recognition. Will I ever get my turn in the spotlight? Will anybody ever know or care who I am?

Fame! The glitzy allurement for all ego! It is never wholesome, and it is always demanding. It is a powerful and all-consuming fire. The lust for fame changes the church into a theater. It uses the hands for applause, the same hands that should be lifted in prayer. It treasures trifles and scorns humility. Fame lures cheap messiahs who leap from the temple battlements rather than serve their God in the suffering fields of human contagion.

Satan peddles fame as a cure-all for anonymity. My second temptation came largely as a vaudeville play. If I could throw myself down from the pinnacle of the temple and land unhurt, a crowd would gather around the stunt. It would have been so easy to go from anonymity to acrobatic fame.

What my Enemy was really suggesting was that I might substitute the cross for a one-man circus. He was trying to convince me I could get elected Messiah without the ugly necessity of dying. I could trade the humiliation for human applause.

But the whole point of my incarnation was to live life as ordinary people have to live it. No one besides me gets the option of leaping off a spire to become a local hero. If I was going to endure existence for the sake of people, I had to do it the way they had to do it. Fame is the province of few, but pain is sooner or later the province of all. Dying is harder than a publicity stunt. But dying is universal. So I died.

Serve me. Look for no theatrical shortcuts. Learn the art of dying daily. Do not be like those who serve me only as long as it puts them in some arena of applause. Are we together on this? Then turn from applause and embrace integrity. The chains of your temptations once resisted will become the silver cords that bind my soul to yours.

LORD JESUS,
what is the lure in fame?
What is the lure in wanting everyone to know who I am?
Why cannot I be content to be anonymous?
Why am I not willing to be less,
that you may be more?

Forgive my need to lead some grand parade,
to leap, unharmed, the temple balustrade.
Amen.

13

I WANT TO BE THE BOSS

MATTHEW 4:8-10
Again, the devil took Him to a very high mountain, and showed Him all the kingdoms of the world, and their glory; and He said to Him, "All these things will I give You, if You fall down and worship me." Then Jesus said to him, "Begone, Satan! For it is written, 'You shall worship the Lord your God, and serve Him only.'"

LORD, help! I am the low soul on the corporate totem pole. I'm tired of being bossed around. I want to be the boss for a change. Is it so wrong to want to run things—at least for a little while?

Power can be glorious. How easily you can be drawn into its subtle web. The day the Tempter showed me all the kingdoms of the world, it occurred to me how much good a world ruler might do. Surely every tyrant at first saw only the good that might be done. But the current history of the planet is the bloody tale of 28 civilizations whose leaders killed and pillaged their way to control. Their power only resulted in blood and death.

Business empires are often led by those who ascended the corporate ladder to claim a noble throne. Yet once they gained the mace of power, they were never quite able to see the throngs around them as real people. Their underlings became mere fodder for their greed.

Satan knows that there is something dark within you that would like to control others. He confronted me in the same way. Therefore he showed me all the nations of the world. The flags of empires were flying! The heads of state were there. I could have instantly been King.

Therein lay the deception.

The way of the kingdom is not the way of empire. God never saves the world all at once. It is his great desire to conquer all of humankind but only at the rate of one soul at a time. Every human being in any time has had but a single desire: to be seen singly.

Observe a child who is trying to tell her distracted father something very important. The father may be paying little attention. Finally, when the child has had enough, she will take her father's broad chin in her chubby little hands and pull his face toward her own. When their eyes are looking into each other's, she will tell her father all she wants him to know.

This is a picture of all that God wants for you in claiming his kingdom. He wants no distraction between himself and you.

Never forget: You too are mine. I love you not as a part of the masses. I love you clearly, apart, separately. I would want you for my subject if no one else ever called me King. Rejoice! You are loved.

You don't need to control others to have meaning. You need only the love of God to endorse your significance.

LORD JESUS,
give me that God-given joy
of enjoying people without controlling them.
I want to walk among people, serving them,
not using them.
I want no power residual in myself.
I want only that power of yours—
that flow-through power
that enables me to minister in your name
but leaves others unable to remember mine.

May I become a channel whose one course
is conduit into a living force.
Amen.

WHEN ANGELS APPLAUD

MATTHEW 4:11
Then the devil left Him; and behold, angels came and began to
minister to Him.

LORD,
is there any real reward in doing the right thing? Do
those who struggle with temptation really win, or do
they live disconsolate that they denied themselves the
pleasures they never owned? Do angels really applaud
their self-control, or do they say, "Loosen up and live"?

Your question is fair. Do angels celebrate your triumph over temptation?

A certain steward was asked by his master to take a business trip into a
far country. The nature of his business was such that he would have much
free time for sexual exploits when he arrived. The coming license of his trip
began to dominate his thinking. He began to anticipate the revelries and
indulgences he would grant himself. Finally he began to swim in his feelings of desire. He saw his own marriage as something trivial that he would
sacrifice to his mental fancies. His children were of no consequence. His
lust was all consuming.

He abandoned his inhibitions and began to stalk his desires. Finally he
willfully contemplated it for all the joy it seemed to promise. The force of
all his intentions at last camped night and day in his soul until the day of
the trip came. It was the force of his faith in me that at last began to speak
to him. He began, at long last, to quit asking what he owed himself and
began asking what he owed God.

At the heart of all he owed God was the issue of righteousness.
Righteousness is the great "I ought to!" When you confront the great "I
ought to," God's answer will not come back to you in a totally satisfying
response. There is always pleasure in sin for a season. But when you ask the
great "I ought to" questions in the presence of God, you get answers in
terms of your ultimate satisfaction and not the immediate. Yes, there will

always be those seasons in your life that are rather barren in terms of ego gratification. Raising children often comes without all the affirmation their parents would like to get. There are times when spouses forget to tell their mates just how much they mean. But when life becomes harsh, the true children of God distinguish themselves by refusing to abandon the only morality that God can honor.

So this story ends well. The steward turned at last to righteousness for its own sake. He learned the only moral truth that matters: It is good to do good because good is the only thing that endures. Such morality is rooted in the hearts of all those whom my Father calls his friends.

And so it was in my life—three times I said no to the Tempter. Then the angels came and ministered to me. The angels do clap their hands. They love to celebrate the victories of ordinary people with extraordinary character. Do well, then listen; the angels are applauding.

LORD JESUS,
I know that I am much more shaped
by what I deny myself
than I am by my indulgences.
The evil things that I allow myself
become the bars
that soon imprison me in compromise.

The apples left in Satan's tempting bowl
are stored in heaven's vaults as fruit of gold.
Amen.

GETTING GOD'S VIEW OF WHO YOU ARE

JOHN 1:19-23

And this is the witness of John, when the Jews sent to him priests and Levites from Jerusalem to ask him, "Who are you?" And he confessed, and did not deny, and he confessed, "I am not the Christ." And they asked him, "What then? Are you Elijah?" And he said, "I am not." "Are you the Prophet?" And he answered, "No." They said then to him, "Who are you, so that we may give an answer to those who sent us? What do you say about yourself?" He said, " I am a voice of one crying in the wilderness, 'Make straight the way of the Lord,' as Isaiah the prophet said."

LORD,
when the philosopher said, "Know thyself," he left me too daunting a task. Sometimes I think I am an achiever. Sometimes I don't. Sometimes I do something noble. Sometimes I don't. Sometimes I deny myself, sometimes I indulge myself. I have no idea who I really am a great deal of the time.

To know yourself is to lose the distinction between what you do and who you are. This had happened to John. More than all else, he desired to please God. As a result, pleasing God became his reason for getting up each morning. Who he was, was hidden in his desire to preach the kingdom.

It would have been so easy for John to have taken for himself the glory he knew was mine. When they asked him if he was the Christ, he could have said, "How nice you noticed," or "You may be sure of it." But the claim never seemed to occur to him. He would not steal my title...not even borrow from my glory.

I am sure that you have never been tempted to call yourself the Christ, but you may have profited by calling yourself Christian. Many politicians don't really revel in the name of Christ, but they have found it politically expedient to be a Christian.

Study John. He never gave the inquiring crowds his own name, for he felt his own name held no significance. This is the sign of true greatness. If you serve me well, you could become well-known for your service. Your name might someday be listed on the marquis beside my own. But let your love for me glorify me. Seek John's wisdom and always give me first place. Love me for my sake as I have loved you for your sake.

To know yourself is to get out of yourself. To get out of yourself is to love someone besides yourself. Get wrapped up in me; forget yourself. All romance frees the lover to center his best affections on his love.

No great husband ever wondered why his wife didn't love him more. He so spent himself in loving that the issue of being loved never occurred to him. So knowing yourself is not a matter of getting your neuroses settled. It is a matter of honest passion—do you genuinely love me?

LORD JESUS,
am I too central in my witness to your excellence?
Do I too quickly pass out my card to those in need?
Do I point to you and say, "Behold the King!"
or rather point to my ego-driven self and ask why the
world doesn't take more of an interest in helping me define myself?

Self-knowledge is at last a pointless thing.
In knowing Christ is hidden everything!
Amen.

16

ECCE AGNUS DEI

JOHN 1:29

The next day he saw Jesus coming to him, and said, "Behold, the
Lamb of God who takes away the sin of the world!"

LORD,
I want to point at you and cry, "Behold the King!" But
when I do, the world seems to cry, "Who cares?" It's hard
to be a salesman when nobody wants the product.

It's true. The world has grown so secular, it sees no need of heralds who
point to me and cry, "Hosanna!" But then grand pronouncements always
seem quaint in little settings. I walked one day into the midst of a largely
rural assemblage. Gathered there were farmers and shepherds and the ordinary poor of Israel. John pointed at me, calling me the universal sacrifice
that would end forever the problem of human sin.

The occasion seemed prosaic, but had you been there you would have
known immediately that this was just the right place to make such an
announcement. John's great pronouncement came at the river Jordan. Here
in this very earthy place, a carpenter and a desert prophet met. The Spirit,
dove-like, came down and marked the spot. And none of the world of that
day understood how cosmic the event really was. None, of course, except
for the shepherds, the farmers, and the poor.

So many times in the Gospels, the four evangelists say that I was moved
with compassion for those in need. It is true. Yet when I met John at the
river, the dove descended. God himself was unmistakably moved with
compassion. There among these simple and needy people he proclaimed
himself as a God who would offer much more than gilt-edged salvation to
the elite in high places.

My Father loves the poor. It is not for their sins only that I died. But God
knows the rich often feel secure in what they own. The poor are far more
prone to find their security in who owns them.

You have done a wonderful thing. It is always proper to point to me and
proclaim my lordship. But those in need are more likely to heed your

proclamation than are the self-reliant. It has been said that only the hurting have a God. Therefore seek that fellowship of neediness where the Spirit descends like a dove. Welcome the Spirit. Then our love for each other will grow from our mutual neediness. I was broken on the cross, and you have been broken by your sinfulness. Our double brokenness delights my Father. When you are on your knees, listen and you will hear the Spirit cry those famous river words, "*Ecce Agnus Dei.* Behold the Lamb of God."

LORD JESUS,
have I accepted my church friends
as though the having of such friends
is the reason I go to church?
Help me to make my church that kind of place
that sees the needy crying for the warmth of God's favor.
I want to be an evangelist who visits all who are in need.
I want to see the dove descending on the hopeless.
I want to cry,

"Behold the Lamb of God! He comes again
to fill your neediness and cleanse your sin."
Amen.

17

MY FRIENDS ARE YOUR
FRIENDS AND WE'RE ALL
GOD'S FRIENDS

JOHN 1:35-42

Again the next day John was standing with two of his disciples, and he looked upon Jesus as He walked, and said, "Behold, the Lamb of God!" And the two disciples heard him speak, and they followed Jesus. And Jesus turned, and beheld them following, and said to them, "What do you seek?" And they said to Him, "Rabbi (which translated means Teacher), where are You staying?" He said to them, "Come, and you will see." They came therefore and saw where He was staying; and they stayed with Him that day, for it was about the tenth hour. One of the two who heard John speak, and followed Him, was Andrew, Simon Peter's brother. He found first his own brother Simon, and said to him, "We have found the Messiah" (which translated means Christ). He brought him to Jesus. Jesus looked at him, and said, "You are Simon the son of John; you shall be called Cephas" (which translated means Peter).

LORD,
I sure do like my friends. I'm so reluctant to share them.

Just how protective are you about your friends? Do you see how freely John gave his disciples to be my own? Now here is his rich example to the church. John must have loved his disciples. How much every teacher's students mean to the teacher. How hurt teachers can become when someone else lures their students away from them. It is hard for you to love your friends and see them give their allegiance to another. It is normal for you to prize the loyalty of your companions. But do not hang little invisible tags on your friends that say "mine." Some have been known to call their employees "my staff" or "my people." Churches can be particularly zealous over their members. They become edgy when they hear that one of their members has joined someone else's church.

John had been waiting all his life to see the Messiah. When it turned out to be me, he proved his allegiance to me by openly allowing his disciples to become mine.

How could I receive those disciples who had meant so much to him, and claim them as my own? It was because John and I were not in business for ourselves. John lived to serve me, and I lived to serve my Father.

This simple truth holds the key to your own happiness: You are not your own; you do not exist to serve yourself. Those friends in your circle of allegiances are not yours. They belong to God. If you try too much to hold on to them, you are destined to feel loss when they move away from you.

"Can those people whom you so readily surrender really mean anything to you?" you may ask. These friends will mean more once you see that both of you are part of God's family. Then you will quit worrying about keeping your friends because you have begun to see them as your family—as brothers and sisters. It's a great comfort really. We rarely worry about losing our family—only our friends.

LORD JESUS,
I must confess my insecurity to you.
I don't feel good about life unless I know
that I own a few friends who are going to be there for me
at those desperate seasons of need.

Help me give up my need to own my friends,
or use a one of them for my own ends.
Amen.

18

A SOMEBODY
FROM NOWHERE

JOHN 1:45-46

Philip found Nathanael and said to him, "We have found Him of whom Moses in the Law and also the Prophets wrote, Jesus of Nazareth, the son of Joseph." And Nathanael said to him, "Can any good thing come out of Nazareth?" Philip said to him, "Come and see."

LORD,
I've crossed no great boundaries to serve you. I hold no elite degrees from great centers of learning. My heritage is not from a bloodline of notables. My family tree contains no great names. I'm a nowhere person. I wish I were somebody from someplace whose status might actually help you in your kingdom.

Give me who you are and forget where you came from. Where I'll take you is so much more important than where you've been.

It is hard for us to believe that great people can come from small addresses. In many cases, great people make the world aware of the unknown, rustic locales from which they came. There are many little places about which we would have never known except for the souls that made them famous.

It is fortunate for Nazareth that I came from there. Otherwise, no one would ever have heard of the place. Now my name is rarely spoken except that Nazareth is referred to as well. Jesus of Nazareth they called me. "Jesus of what?" was Nathaniel's question. "Can anything good come out of Nazareth?" Nathaniel had committed the sin of sanctifying geography. There exist in each of our minds those large places of importance that we have dubbed as sanctified. In these big places we permit God to do big things in big ways. But what of the small towns? What of Nazareth?

You now call me Savior. Where was that bit of nowhere where you found me? Where was your Nazareth? How did God come to you to hallow your nothingness and consecrate your small situation? Did you not, in that small place, learn that wherever God touches life, that place is sacred?

When God called Abraham to come up out of Ur of the Chaldees, he came into new and barren land that was destined to become the Holy Land. It was really no holier than anywhere else. It was just that within its tiny, eastern Mediterranean boundaries, God would in time get involved with all the people of the world. God sanctifies people, not the land. Nonetheless, as Abraham came into the land, he piled up stones and built a little altar. He offered a sacrifice to God. He called the place *Bethel,* or House of God. There was really no house there, only a crude little altar. But Abraham returned to that primitive pile of stones from time to time to remind himself that whatever God touched was holy. Let Abraham's crude altars be a lesson for your life.

Can anything good come out of Nazareth? Of course—I did. But you too came from your own Nazareth. And when I entered you, your Nazareth, like mine, held the fullest possibility of God. What will be remembered of you? Just this. I was in your life. I owned you. Your land, your life, your career—all these were holy. Good things do come out of Nazareth!

LORD JESUS,
*you made the names of Bethlehem and Nazareth
household words.
It was because you were so submitted to your Father's will
that your perfect execution of all that he had called you to do
redeemed the entire globe and left these two little pinpoints of geography
with great significance.*

*Help me by my supreme obedience
to give each place I touch significance.
Amen.*

MIRROR OF TOMORROW

JOHN 1:48-50

Nathanael said to Him, "How do You know me?" Jesus answered and said to him, "Before Philip called you, when you were under the fig tree, I saw you." Nathanael answered Him, "Rabbi, You are the Son of God; You are the King of Israel." Jesus answered and said to him, "Because I said to you that I saw you under the fig tree, do you believe? You shall see greater things than these."

LORD,
I see nothing of real importance in my life. Can you see more in me than I see in myself?

I can see so much more in your life than you will ever see. You see only the "as is." I see the "not yets" of your life. You read your life by the dim, current light. I read your life against the brightness of God's tomorrow. You see your life slogging through the high and obscuring weeds of the moment. I see you crowned with the laurels of your achievements.

When I first saw Nathanael, he was under the fig tree, lost in wondering about who the Messiah would be. Then all of a sudden he met me. Even as he did, I reminded him of all that he had been considering in his fig-tree reverie. He was amazed. I had been looking into his soul. When he grasped my unknown probings, he was overwhelmed with wonder.

I had to remind him that reading his mind was a simple wonder. I called him into discipleship. If anything about my disciples amazed me, it was that they were so easily amazed. I want you to learn from Andrew. In following the course of God, you must prepare yourself for an emerging life of wonder. You cannot get mixed up with God and live an ordinary and predictable life.

This is the beauty of the redeemed life: *New* becomes a common word. When you think you are beginning to grasp what might be expected, everything becomes unexpected. Just when you think the sun comes up in the east, it comes up in the south, and you are left trying to explain the extraordinary acts of God in vain.

Follow me, but watch where you step, for your lowly path may suddenly become the footbridge over exhilarating heights.

Nathaniel's amazement is the first musing of every childish Christian. If you have me in your life and still find your life unachieving, get honest and despise the inconsistency. Get ready for the splendor. I am your Lord. Your ordinary living was over the moment you received me into your life.

When first we met I gave you the mirror of tomorrow. Throw away the older glasses—they are filmed over with the dull reflections of some previous, useless moments. I live inside you, so prepare your hallelujahs. Joy comes in seeing what you can be, never in seeing what you are.

LORD JESUS,
I have sinned so much of my life,
claiming to follow a Christ who can do anything
and yet remaining ever so content
to see you do almost nothing.
There has often been so little of wonder in my ordinary life,
that I have caused people only to see an ordinary Christ.

Forgive me, therefore, for each humdrum hour,
my weak todays, my loss of future power!
Amen.

20

THE PEOPLE'S GOSPEL

JOHN 2:1-5

And on the third day there was a wedding in Cana of Galilee, and the mother of Jesus was there; and Jesus also was invited, and His disciples, to the wedding. And when the wine gave out, the mother of Jesus said to Him, "They have no wine." And Jesus said to her, "Woman, what do I have to do with you? My hour has not yet come." His mother said to the servants, "Whatever He says to you do it."

LORD,
the philosopher has said that "hell is other people." It seems that people are always in the way of all I want to do or be. I've had a tyrannical boss, my carping critics, the annoying bill collectors. People are always vying to take my position or one-up me in some endeavor. Are you sure you want me to love everyone?

You need a new view of people. See them as they really are. They are the soul of all that God's love is about. Sociology is God's favorite science. I first felt the importance of all people in a country wedding at the little town of Cana of Galilee.

The wedding feast went on long after the wine gave out. My disciples and I were part of the reason that the host ran short of wine in the first place. You cannot expand the guest list to include 13 hungry, thirsty men and not run the risk of a social catastrophe. So, considering that the wine shortage was partly our fault, and considering that my mother had told the hostess she could count on me to ease the situation, I did it. Theologians have long objected to this "water made wine" miracle. It always seems to them that my first miracle should have been one more related to human meaning—an exorcism, a healing, a storm calming.

But it was not to be.

The first of all my mighty works had to do with simple, good sociology: My mother's friends were out of wine. By the host's own admission they had drunk plenty already. Still, propriety owned the day. I made the wine for my mother and her friends, 120 gallons or so. It was a large wedding. I didn't save any souls, but I did save several things: I saved my mother's reputation with her friends, and I saved the host the embarrassment of appearing that he had been too cheap to order enough wine.

This first miracle of warm sociology forever focused on the importance that people hold for God. Why then does this first miracle befuddle so many Christians? Some who overemphasize temperance would have much preferred that I change wine into water.

And to some extent I agreed with those critical theologians: This water-to-wine miracle does not hold the immense meaning of my later miracles. But it does make a theological statement that cannot be denied. My Father loves people. So I made water—humble water—serve the moment. I made wine. Good wine. All agreed.

But then you'd expect it to be good wine, for all that God does is done well. I've never gotten through changing drab things into better stuff. Are your own social ills ever unmanageable? Have you chewed all the good out of life? I'm the master repairer of needy sociology. Bring me the watery weakness of all your interrelationships. Now dip into that insipid water. See, there is sweetness. Behold—there is life. The wine is good.

LORD JESUS,
help me to love people so much
that I move through life noticing
where I might be of help.
What little things could I do?
Hold a door? Take a casserole to the sick?
Bake a loaf of bread for the hungry?

Where is that Cana my poor life might find,
where is the water I might change to wine?
Amen.

21

TO HALLOW THE HUMDRUM

JOHN 2:11
This beginning of His signs Jesus did in Cana of Galilee, and mani-
fested His glory, and His disciples believed in Him.

LORD,
mediocrity is in charge of my life too often. I have the
blahs, all in capitol letters: B-L-A-H-S. What happens to
us that causes our post-conversion excitement to sour?
Some humdrum spigot has emptied our souls of the
sweet life. Where is the joy that I had when I first knew
you?

Remember this: Blah is just the flip side of the undisciplined life. Blah
is just the water you never ordered to be wine. I made wine from water
simply because the water realized it had a Maker and a Master. Make this
a metaphor for your own life.

As a likeness of the kingdom, this first miracle is significant for you. My
power holds the potential for change in your life. Water is more than water
at my command. The plain is ornate if I order it to be. The humdrum is
festive!

I was often criticized by the Pharisees for being a "glutton and a
winebibber" (Matthew 11:19). They criticized me because I went to parties.
Their criticism was meant to be a put-down, but parties really represent
the best opportunity of God. Lonely people come to parties looking for
relationships. Despondent people come to parties looking for a good time.
Hungry people come to parties looking for something to eat. People often
meet their lifetime mates at parties. Wherever you find a party in progress,
my Father is there.

Is your life blah? Water tends to be blah.

Consider how much greater is the value of wine over water. Water may
slake the thirst, but wine incites it. Water cannot excite the mind and make
it heady with adventure, but wine can. Water cannot make the timid bold,
but wine pricks the courage. Wine has the power to elicit stimulating
conversations from the most socially inept.

Can you see why on the Day of Pentecost, the crowd of foreigners thought that the disciples had all been up late with new wine? The Spirit raged, and his inebriating reality emboldened the timid church to go into the streets. It was drunkenness of a kind. They were inebriated with heaven. They were the first to see that the Spirit had brought the church out of her withdrawn solitude into the joyous marketplace.

How long have the blahs defined you?

How long has it been since your innate joy has caused anyone to accuse you of being full of new wine? Have you claimed to be filled with me and sometimes lived a dull, humdrum existence? There is one other great attribute of wine. Wine holds the power of a delicious addiction. Are you living in that glorious state of spiritual inebriation that addicts you to me? Do you, in hopeless inebriation, thirst more and more for my presence in your life? Please, the kingdom of God really is a party. Hats and whistles and joyous purpose. Come to the excitement. Celebrate the heady joy of our friendship. Let the taste of new wine be a continuous miracle of joy in your life.

LORD JESUS,
here I am, so often weak and watery
in my witness.
I am so often so tasteless and so bland in my walk with you
that I make you appear bland as well.
Consecrate my thin enthusiasm and change me
into the dangerous and exciting
disciple you want me to be.

Please come and change my aqueous salvation
to heady, happy, bold intoxication.
Amen.

22

MARKETPLACE CHRISTIANS

JOHN 2:13-17

And the Passover of the Jews was at hand, and Jesus went up to Jerusalem. And He found in the temple those who were selling oxen and sheep and doves, and the moneychangers seated. And He made a scourge of cords, and drove them all out of the temple, with the sheep and the oxen; and He poured out the coins of the moneychangers, and overturned their tables; and to those who were selling the doves He said, "Take these things away; stop making My Father's house a house of merchandise." His disciples remembered that it was written, "Zeal for Thy house will consume me."

LORD,
I don't care if you give me a Mercedes-Benz, but how about a little place in the Christian yellow pages? I want to serve God, but more like a professional concert artist or traveling evangelist. So many people are serving you while they make a living. What's wrong with a little "God.com" anyway?

You're right about this, of course. But beware of greed. Many have learned to spell the word *Savior* with a dollar sign—*$avior*.

God is good for business. Those in the first century who bought and sold oxen to pilgrims appeared on the surface to be doing worshippers a favor. Those who had journeyed a long way—often from distant provinces—could not bring their altar sacrifices all that way. Those who came from closer locales were often merchants or lawyers and were too "citified" to raise their own sacrificial animals. These temple merchants served all Jews by selling oxen that the wealthy could buy for sacrifice. They also kept sheep for the moderately wealthy and doves for the very poor.

While it appeared to be a thoughtful little business to help those who had no livestock of their own, the temple merchants were making extravagant livings by offering these animals for sale. Many of them wrangled to try and outsell the other vendors who were also hawking their bleating, mooing, cooing wares. They had done it for a long time. They had gotten used to making money in the house of the Lord. Candidly they joked among themselves that they were getting rich off the sins of those people whose iniquities required their sacrificial animals.

The church has always known its profiteers. But in your own heart, resolve never to use your brothers and sisters in the faith. Never bring your own wares into the house of God to make the church your own private marketplace instead of the temple God intends it to be.

Has your church ever been a courtyard where some believers hawk their self-interest? I have no whip of small cords to drive self-interest from the greedy hearts of modern-day worship centers. Therefore I encourage you to purge your own motives. Bring me the sacrifice of your heart each week. You will find me when you seek me with all your heart.

LORD JESUS,
*help me not to pursue self-interest
in the guise of worshiping you.
Help me, rather, to come to the altar,
not with something to sell but eager to spend all I am to buy
your complete lordship in my life.*

*Your altar is the place I spend my soul,
lay down caprice to purchase your control.
Amen.*

THE PROCESS OF LEARNING THE TRUTH

JOHN 2:18-22

The Jews therefore answered and said to Him, "What sign do You show to us, seeing that You do these things?" Jesus answered and said to them, "Destroy this temple, and in three days I will raise it up." The Jews therefore said, "It took forty-six years to build this temple, and will You raise it up in three days?" But He was speaking of the temple of His body. When therefore He was raised from the dead, His disciples remembered that He said this; and they believed the Scripture, and the word which Jesus had spoken.

LORD,
I want to believe that heaven's on the way, but I am floundering in doubt. It just seems that life is the sum total of all my weak attempts to make it meaningful. I would like to believe that glory is possible, that your power can order my weakness to find itself alive with a vital strength.

You are not alone in your need to see more miracles in life. Everyone wants me to put a little more "super" into their "natural." But I am truth—personal truth, almighty truth, miraculous truth. Still, not all truth comes to us by rote, like the memorization of mathematical tables. The leaders of the Jews were naturally outraged that I should drive them from the temple for merchandising animals. They wanted to know by whose authority I had taken so audacious a step. They were literally asking, "Who do you think you are?" I knew who I was, but I knew they would never believe me if I came right out and said it. So I decided to speak to them with a kind of truth that would only reveal itself in the process of time.

"Destroy *this* temple," I said, pointing to my own body, "and I will raise it in three days." My words eluded them. Even as I said it, they looked not at me; they looked outward upon the magnificent temple, which they had profaned in the merchandising of their animals. They reminded me that it had taken nearly half a century to build that temple. I smiled. The sheer glory of my doubled meaning would gradually emerge as a greater truth than they could imagine. Still, the disciples, while puzzled over exactly what I meant, marked the statement and stored it away for later examination.

There was little good that day in trying to make the Jewish leaders understand the marvelous truth that was on the way. And the disciples themselves were so new at all my teachings that the glory of the resurrection still lay beyond their understanding. But afterward, they remembered the savory glory of things yet untasted. Delightfully then, they relived the taste of all my promises.

So if you want a sign to help you believe in my extraordinary power, remember this: The day is already coming when all you thought you knew of me will be heightened by my second coming. You will arrive in heaven. Then you will taste at last what you have up till now sometimes doubted. The full reality of heaven will then be so much more than you have ever imagined.

LORD JESUS,
I come to you befuddled by weakness.
I know that what is on the way is so much more than I have imagined.

I trust that when I see it all, I'll see
how power invades my disabilities.
Amen.

PREPARING YOURSELF TO DEAL WITH FICKLE COMMITMENT

JOHN 2:23-25

Now when He was in Jerusalem at the Passover, during the feast, many believed in His name, beholding His signs which He was doing. But Jesus, on His part, was not entrusting Himself to them, for He knew all men, and because He did not need anyone to bear witness concerning man for He Himself knew what was in man.

LORD,
I've been stabbed in the back by someone I trusted. Why?

Are you angry because you were stabbed or because it was in the back? You have two questions here. Here are my two answers. You were stabbed because of the nature of man—man is a traitor. Trust me in this matter. People can hail you as a victor on Palm Sunday and make you a victim on Maundy Thursday.

But if you're asking why it was in the back, please try to remember, few people have ever been stabbed in the front! Head-on is too audacious, too visible.

Judas taught me this.

Treachery is rarely frontal in its attack. The back is the place for the stabbing. Human nature at its best is a mixture of reliability and treachery. Remember, you yourself are not free of guilt in this matter. If you doubt this, think of those times when you have disappointed someone else because you found yourself breaking oaths you fully intended to keep.

In everyone's life there come times of high elation. At the outset of my ministry I experienced such a time in Jerusalem. Because of the miracles I had done, there was a rich harvest of disciples. Reports of my teaching ministry were glowing and positive. My followers were basking in the warm glow of my early success. They promised me their loyalty, and their promises were as yet untarnished by their later betrayals.

So when they came up to me to pat me on the back and say, "Good show, Jesus!" I smiled warmly at them. I breathed a prayer to my Father, that he would see them through their giddy and flighty loyalty when the real showdown came. You must trust your brothers and sisters, but remember, even your finest Christian friends are only one sin away from betrayal and abandonment. Therefore be wise.

Love me supremely. Trust me completely. Never give this same whole-hearted trust to anyone else. I will never leave you nor forsake you (Hebrews 13:5). Others may. All things are possible only through me (Mark 10:27), not through others. My God will supply all your needs according to his riches in glory (Philippians 4:19). There is no such promise living even in the very finest people in the church.

These were the reasons that I committed myself to no one. I knew that in spite of their good intentions they were all capable of betrayal. Thus I lived with a kind of realism that Good Friday could not surprise. When you experience killing hurt, it is often because you accorded mere Christians the steadfast faithfulness you should have given to me alone.

LORD JESUS,
I want to shield myself from that dissolution
of soul that comes from giving
more trust to my fellow believers
than their fallen natures could ever permit them to keep.
Help me not to shield myself from hurt that others will
give me from time to time.

I'll give myself to all and not in part
for treachery may camp in any heart.
Amen.

25

ON BEING BORN

JOHN 3:1-7

Now there was a man of the Pharisees, named Nicodemus, a ruler of the Jews; this man came to Him by night, and said to Him, "Rabbi, we know that You have come from God as a teacher; for no one can do these signs that You do unless God is with him." Jesus answered and said to him, "Truly, truly, I say to you, unless one is born again, he cannot see the kingdom of God." Nicodemus said to Him, "How can a man be born when he is old? He cannot enter a second time into his mother's womb and be born, can he?" Jesus answered, "Truly, truly, I say to you, unless one is born of water and the Spirit, he cannot enter into the kingdom of God. That which is born of the flesh is flesh, and that which is born of the Spirit is spirit. Do not marvel that I said to you, 'You must be born again.'"

LORD,
I want to start over. I think I could do things better if I could start over. If only I could turn back the clock and erase my wasted opportunities, I would be able to live the life I wish I were living.

I have good news for you: "Do overs" are possible! Life can begin again.
It is not uncommon for people in severely distraught emotional states to say, "I wish I were dead." Such depressive statements often come from those who really are dead in trespasses and sin. They are dead to every possibility of all that my Father would like to make of them. They are often dead to hope. They are dead to honest dreams of living a meaningful life. They seem never to have heard the good news that God is the God of second chances. Life knows no terminal despair. Anyone can start over.
The ugly crush of life can lash you to the skeletons of your failures. But consider the wonder of birth for a moment. A little human form issues from the birth canal. The birth fluids are cleaned away. The umbilical is cut, and independent life has come to be.

At such a moment, no one talks about how poorly this newborn child may someday turn out. Rather, in these highly positive beginnings there is much talk of all that will be. All is hope. All is glory. People bring presents, parties flourish.

But with maturity comes harsh reality.

The joy of birth is eclipsed by the long, long process of dying.

Enter life!

Enter pain!

Enter suicide!

Can you see the glory of what I said to Nicodemus? He could start over. You can too. You literally can be *born again*. You can abandon a dreary existence and find a place of glorious beginning. I can live my life through you, touching all your failure with hope. To be born of the Spirit is life everlasting. To be born again is not life after death. It is life instead of death. It will bear you to the Father to live in his presence forever. It is simple logic to choose life. So choose it. Be born again. Embrace the Spirit. Start over.

LORD JESUS,
I choose to live forever.
I choose to reject my sole love for mere physical life,
which may sometimes be noble
but is never eternal.

I choose that life begotten from above;
I'm born again in everlasting love.
Amen.

26

HONOR THE WIND

The wind blows where it wishes and you hear the sound of it, but do not know where it comes from or where it is going; so is everyone who is born of the Spirit.

LORD, is it possible to tap into undying vitality? Why are we who say you are our God so often the very picture of defeat? I go to church seeking a fellowship of life and vitality, and so often I see only hollow souls who live dull and spiritless lives. I want to dwell among a people who are alive with destiny and vitality.

There is an answer to your need. The Spirit! He is the wind. Wind is the emblem of the Spirit, and the Spirit makes possible my indwelling presence. In some ways, wind is the best symbol for God himself. In the Old Testament, God first committed himself to the heroes of the faith under the name Yahweh. This breathy word for God was likely at first also a form of the word for *being*. To say this word, Yahweh, calls to remembrance the wind. Was it not this Yahweh wind that Israel felt in the stinging sands of Sinai? Was it not in the howling desert gales that Israel felt God as he moved all about them? Was not this Yahweh the stormy God who blew through Israel as she lived out her frail and needy existence in the deserts of the Exodus?

The wind blew, and God was there. He could be felt! He could be seen when the proud banners of Israel's legions floated on his breath. The wind was evidence of his providence, for it carried the manna and quail. The wind was evidence of his power, for it flattened their frail tents and made them cower among the splitting rocks. Wind came, and God came and ordered nature. He blew, the clouds scattered, and the sun came.

Consider the power of this joyous, moving symbol. Stand upon a sea cliff with the wind in your face. And as sure as you know there is wind in this high and lofty exhilaration, know that I want to be a moving and invisible force in your life.

If you only knew the force I have shut up in your soul.

This is the breath of the Holy Spirit, in which you were born again.

He blew, and your addictions confessed themselves and fled before his power. He blew, and your doubt died as you openly cried out that you belonged to God. The never-ending stirring of this wind is my gift to you. It is my earthly indwelling self. I am the wind, heart sized and powerful, as fierce and glorious as the storms of Sinai.

This wind can set you free to witness with such power that the world around you will celebrate me. You have but to fall on your knees and bow your head. Then you will know the full force of that inner stirring that I have given to you. Then vitality will move into your church.

But the church is not its keeper—you are. You have no right to expect the church to give you the vitality because you think you need it. No. You don't go to church to get the wind; you take the wind with you into your church. By doing this you bring life to your church. It never works the other way around. Celebrate the wind. It is your gift to share with this dull and plodding planet.

LORD JESUS,
I am in awe of your invisible stronghold.
I know you are there as I know the wind exists.
Blow on me, Spirit of God.

Fill me with your holy breath divine
and whisper in the wind that you are mine.
Amen.

THE FOLLY OF UNYIELDING ARROGANCE

JOHN 3:13-15

And no one has ascended into heaven, but He who descended from heaven, even the Son of Man. And as Moses lifted up the serpent in the wilderness, even so must the Son of Man be lifted up; that whoever believes may in Him have eternal life.

LORD, why is it so hard for me to admit my sins? I want God's forgiveness, but I hate having to abase myself to obtain it.

Pride is the foe of your confession. To confess your sin, you must first confess your self-righteousness.

In Sinai during the Exodus, the fiery serpents came. They stung the people for their arrogant complaints against my Father. But after the people were bitten, God told Moses to make a brass serpent and put it on a pole. With God's judgment came a simple requirement: Those who were bitten had only to look at the brass snake to live. It was hard for many of them to admit that they had sinned against God. Some were hard of heart and died rather than confess.

Remember this: Pride always wants to do things on its own. Your pride is but the dingy garment of your ego. Pride is your naked self, pretending to be well dressed. Pride is the great unthinkable wall between God's redemption and your own foolish attempt to provide your own salvation.

Repentance, on the other hand, is the grand work you must do to learn the art of humility. Repentance unstops the ears of your rebellion so you can hear God shout his saving promise, "Look and live!"

It was my Father's will that my cross be lifted up. It carried a joyous and a bitter requirement. Anyone may look and live. But most will die holding their proud faces away from my compassion. Here is history's great deciding point. Peasants have clamped their eyes shut, refusing to look, and they have died. But honest kings have come to the brass serpent and dropped their foolish cankered crowns and lived.

The serpent on the pole is the milepost of my grace for all of those willing to taste its sweet refreshing. Now I ask you, is not my Father wonderful? Won't you scrub away the scales of your pride? Will you not taste his everlasting forgiveness? Will you not come to him yielded and in love? Will you not seek him while your own need is great? The dying sunlight is now falling upon the golden snake. Your entire life can be born anew, as new as the metallic light on a brazen serpent. Bow your head. Turn and look. See! You're alive forevermore! Do not be surprised. Living always begins with looking.

LORD JESUS,
teach me the glory of looking on the serpent,
I was not weaned from pride by just one look.
It comes to me again and again.
My heart is made haughty by a single compliment.
I am made to celebrate my own pitiful reputation
at any passing accolade.
Pride is too much my hardened shell,

so please bid me daily look and be made whole.
Please! Never take the serpent from the pole.
Amen.

28

THERE IS ONLY ONE LORD

JOHN 3:25-30

There arose therefore a discussion on the part of John's disciples with a Jew about purification. And they came to John and said to him, "Rabbi, He who was with you beyond Jordan, to whom you have borne witness, behold, He is baptizing, and all are coming to Him." John answered and said, "A man can receive nothing, unless it has been given him from heaven. You yourselves bear me witness, that I said, 'I am not the Christ,' but, 'I have been sent before Him.' He who has the bride is the bridegroom; but the friend of the bridegroom, who stands and hears him, rejoices greatly because of the bridegroom's voice. And so this joy of mine has been made full. He must increase, but I must decrease."

LORD, I've just been elected. I have won the prize. They put my picture in the paper. I feel just great! I want to give you all the glory for my success, but...well, I just couldn't bring myself to say, "I owe it all to Jesus." After all, there were a lot of important people there. Many congratulating me! I sure feel great!

Beware elation. It neither lives long nor is honest in its deportment. Most people only enjoy playing god when their lives are so secure they have no need of any god beyond themselves.

John's disciples knew this. They were not able to make a smooth transition from exalting their former master to exalting me. Thus they found their original pride languishing in the sloughs of bruised egos. Giving up the limelight is difficult. They had known the wonderful exhilaration of being center stage. Now my disciples were taking that enviable center of reputation.

John reminded his disciples of what they had known all along. Their ministry had only existed to exalt me. Now they were unable to allow me my rightful place as Lord of the church. John made it clear to his followers that when I began my public ministry, his was over.

John knew that the church could only have one Lord. He knew that Lord was me. The church is my bride, and I am her bridegroom. As a member of my church, you are part of my chosen bride. I am your sovereign groom. I alone. Never swagger or boast about your personal accomplishments within my church. I bought you with a love that has never since been measured. Put a little wisdom into your own elation. Your little successes will not bind you to me as fast as a season of brokenness. But such a season is already headed for your life. Don't begrudge its coming. We will meet together as common, wounded lovers when it arrives.

Here is the glorious testament of my kinsman, John: "He must increase, I must decrease." Learn this marvelous phrase. It purges the kingdom of any possibility of human arrogance. In such a continuing confession, Pentecost will fall upon you with every sunrise.

LORD JESUS,
I am in need of that generosity of spirit
that frees everyone—all my friends—
to have their own affair with you.
I want to let them relate to you
all in their own way with their own priorities.

I love you, Lord, so may I never cease
to ask that I decline and you increase.
Amen.

NEXT STOP, SAMARIA

JOHN 4:1-4
When therefore the Lord knew that the Pharisees had heard that Jesus was making and baptizing more disciples than John (although Jesus Himself was not baptizing, but His disciples were), He left Judea, and departed again into Galilee. And He had to pass through Samaria.

LORD, Samaria is that dull land where live those people I can't stand. It is the capital city of all my prejudices. Samaritans are so different. Not noble! Not highborn! Not like me. They're so hoi polloi, so gutteral, so countercultural. Who could ever learn to like Samaritans?

Prejudice is a human foible. Beware of it. It is a state far separate from your own affair with God.

Galilee lies directly north of Jerusalem. The distance between these two places is not great, but between the two lies Samaria. It would have been a simple matter for all Jewish sojourners to travel directly south from Galilee to reach Jerusalem, but most Jews in my day made the trip by taking the trans-Jordan road. They walked all the way around Samaria so they would not have to go through it. Jews and Samaritans didn't much care for each other.

Does this sound like anyone you know?

Jews and Samaritans had distinct and separate worship facilities as well. They both worshipped the same God but were both equally convinced that God liked them best. They rarely spoke favorably about each other to God, and they never talked to God out loud in each other's presence.

John wrote of me that I had to go through Samaria. A strange compulsion was on me. What was this compulsion? My Father's love.

At the well in Sychar I met a Samaritan woman and asked her for a drink. In a world where there were separate drinking places for Jews and Samaritans, she was surprised I even talked to her. She gradually entered into conversation with me. It was a highly self-protective talk and not all that honest. This did not surprise me.

The woman at the well had been married in succession to several men, and the man with whom she was currently living was not her husband. As she examined the water of life that I gave her, she drank it and received life eternal. And after having a drink herself, she made her way quickly back to her village. We stayed there several days, evangelizing among her friends. In fact, a revival broke out around her open acknowledgment of her sins.

True revivals always begin with such confessions. Are you in bondage to some confining prejudice? I know outwardly that you would say no, for it is fashionable among Christians to deny their inner biases. But I beg you to remember that God is in love with all people. He loves those people beyond your favorite color or race or socioeconomic group. Go find yourself a gathering of people who are not like you but do need me.

But you must go where they are. Samaritans never came to Jewish wells for water. So you will have to go to them. Then love them as God loves them. If you want to bring life to a dead world, go and perch yourself on the edge of some needy well and wait. Make yourself available to your world, and the lost will come to you. The water will flow as life.

LORD JESUS,
cleanse all my prejudice away.
I want to feel the great "have to's" of Christian compulsion.
You "had to" go through Samaria,
for there was a needy woman from a needy community,
and without that all-important "have to"
that brought you there,
your Father's fullest work would not get done.

Give me Samarias I must pass through;
show me the saving work that I must do.
Amen.

DANGEROUS TRUTH

LUKE 3:19-20
But when Herod the tetrarch was reproved by him on account of Herodias, his brother's wife, and on account of all the wicked things which Herod had done, he added this also to them all, that he locked John up in prison.

LORD,
I cannot divide the world into two kinds of sins, but I'm afraid I have divided the world into two kinds of truth: convenient truth and dangerous truth. Convenient truth is rarely dangerous, and dangerous truth is rarely convenient. Martyrs are not people who want to die; they are only people who have decided to tell the truth even when it is not convenient.

Integrity is gold kept in the vaults of heaven. Telling the truth can be costly. But truth is a trait of the real messengers of God. When you tell the truth, you will be blessed by all that God blesses. You will be repulsed by all that repulses God. Your value system will be rooted in his holiness. You will not change the subject, and you will not change your mind.

It was such a fervent commitment to righteousness that got John in trouble with the crown. Adultery is wrong. Everyone in any age has known that. But high-level adultery is often winked at. Adulterers with enough civil power are rarely criticized at all for their license. John, like the God he adored, had but one way of treating all people: He denounced all sin as sin. John knew that to tell the truth is hazardous. It is the stuff of crucifixions.

How much are you like John? You are living in a secularized world. As secularism advances, you may find civil law is hammering at your values. These faithless forces in your world will daily put pressure on you to conform to convenience and avoid the dangerous.

John's word to you is this: Never yield your convictions to civil pressure. You are a citizen of two kingdoms. Live and enjoy both of them. But if ever the civil kingdom makes laws that force you to live outside your

Christian principles, remember the example of John the Baptizer. He stood for God and thus lost both his status and his life. Your commitment should be no less.

When they led John the Baptist to the block and took his head, he did not die in panic or fear. He died in confident joy that he had clearly fulfilled his mandate from God. In such a state he stepped from Herod's executioners into the presence of angels. Eternal life is the final confident step of all whose faith keeps courage with confidence.

So do not content yourself with the easy truths. Take hold of those truths that may in time raise a cross that you must die on. Of course, this is not my first will for you. But the servant is not greater than his Lord. Truth was my business. Now it is yours.

LORD JESUS,
real truth extracts a price
in places where godless lies determine moral values.
When human congresses decide what's true
and what is not,
the ancient truth can become too stern a mandate
for the uncommitted world to honor.
Then those who stand for godly truth
become fodder for the consuming fires of secular advance.

Help me to stand for what I know is right,
refuse the dark that's stalked by moral light.
Amen.

31

YOUR WORK IS YOUR INTERRUPTIONS

JOHN 4:7-9

There came a woman of Samaria to draw water. Jesus said to her, "Give Me a drink." For His disciples had gone away into the city to buy food. The Samaritan woman therefore said to Him, "How is it that You, being a Jew, ask me for a drink since I am a Samaritan woman?" (For Jews have no dealings with Samaritans.)

LORD, someday when life slows down, I'm going to serve you full-time. But right now, whatever I try to do, I find I just keep getting interrupted. People are always barging in on my quiet time. Just when I think the day is mine to give to you, the interruptions start. What right do people have to keep interrupting me when I'm trying to be so devout?

I interrupted a woman at the Sychar well. I was a foreigner, a Jew, and I spoke directly to the Samaritan. The prejudice between her people and mine dated back centuries to the time of the exile. Samaritans were half-breeds that had come from the illicit unions of Jews and Canaanites. These half-breeds lived in the contempt of those Jews whose bloodlines remained pure.

Prejudice is the dark art of hating those our community agrees to call outsiders. It may seem that my asking for a drink was a very small thing. But my simple request for water was an affront to convention. The very idea that I would ask a Samaritan woman for a drink from her dipper was repulsive and inappropriate.

But an even worse taboo was violated. I had presumed upon her personal and private agenda. I had interrupted her and required something of her. What right did I have to do such a thing? My right lay in my office as the Savior of the world. To bring salvation to anyone presumes the right to interrupt their workaday habits. You too have this right to interrupt those outside of my love by reminding them of God's agenda for their lives.

You have the right to rescue the perishing. Do not therefore be intimidated by those who curse you or ask you, "What business do you have prying into my private affairs?" The right of rescue is yours.

But to those who reject my sacrifice, God can guarantee no happiness. He is their Creator, and he agonizes over their determination to perish outside his saving love. But the right to choose is theirs. That is why he gives you the permission to interrupt them. This interruption is a saving interruption. It is not a sin to cry "Fire!" in a burning theater. In fact, it is a sin not to. You have the right, even the obligation, to presume upon people's private enjoyment of a play to call out to them for their own sake.

This is the desperate and joyous work you took up when you took up my calling.

LORD JESUS,
there is but one worthy reason
we who love you can presume upon private schedules:
the divine imposition.
We do have the right to cry "Fire!" in any theater—
even in the midst of the most engrossing film.
We are called to deliver the message entrusted to us.
To interrupt the world requires a kind of courage.
It is a courage that invades the trivia of existence
with the imperative of life.

We must feel free to call into the fray,
"Please, sir, God needs a minute of your day."
Amen.

32

THE UNQUENCHABLE THIRST

JOHN 4:11-15

She said to Him, "Sir, You have nothing to draw with and the well is deep; where then do You get that living water? You are not greater than our father Jacob, are You, who gave us the well, and drank of it himself, and his sons, and his cattle?" Jesus answered and said to her, "Everyone who drinks of this water shall thirst again; but whoever drinks of the water that I shall give him shall never thirst; but the water that I shall give him shall become in him a well of water springing up to eternal life."

The woman said to Him, "Sir, give me this water, so I will not be thirsty, nor come all the way here to draw."

LORD,
I want to lead others to love you, but they are so reluctant to come. You know the proverb: You can lead a horse to water, but you can't make him drink.

Drinking cannot be forced. It is a natural consequence of thirst.

Within every heart there is an emptiness that only I can fill. Only once does the Bible bring up the subject of atheism, and on the occasion it is the poet who counsels, "The fool hath said in his heart, There is no God" (Psalm 53:1 KJV). The Bible is silent on the subject because the very notion of atheism is too unthinkably absurd to waste time on. But for all its absurdity, atheists more than all else seem to talk incessantly about the God they don't believe in. They cannot stop fondling their intrigue with the idea of God. Why can they not stop talking about the God they can't accept? Because human beings are innate believers. They all thirst whether or not they say they believe in water.

Never fear the argument of atheists. Never be afraid of those on the other side of the issue who are overly open about God. People back away from those who bring up the issue of God too suddenly and fiercely. Fanaticism—right or left—frightens all those it wants to convert. Appear to all you wish to persuade to be a dedicated but casual lover of God. Those who are considering Christianity want even the most ardent disciples to start out gently when they talk about God. Let them bring up the matter of the weather first. Is it unseasonably warm? Is the humidity high? Will it continue dry on the morrow? But please, not too much of God too soon after your casual hello.

My conversation with the Samaritan woman proves the point. She had to be goaded into a conversation about God. Once into it, however, she hurried eagerly to the issue.

Do you want to tell others about me? Can you get into the conversation with enough finesse to open people up rather than close them down? Tread softly. Begin gently. I asked the Samaritan, "Could I have a drink?" This is, of course, a better place to start than had I said, "Aha, sweet lady, I perceive that you are a multiple divorcée with a huge self-image problem. Get right with God before he strikes you dead and you perish in this well. After that there's fire forever, you know."

People have used such harsh tactics too often as it is. Remember this: Everybody is thirsty for living water. But you must let them have it one dipper at a time. Never throw them into the well.

My kingdom is blessed by these two truths. First, everybody's thirsty. Second, it is best to offer the water of life in such attractive ways that people long to drink it.

LORD JESUS,
there is in every heart
an empty cup,
longing to be filled with the clean, pure,
drinkable grace.

I, therefore, bring my cup to your high shelf,
and beg you fill it daily with yourself.
Amen.

33

THE TEMPLE OF THE HEART

JOHN 4:19-21
The woman said to Him, "Sir, I perceive that You are a prophet.
Our fathers worshiped in this mountain, and you people say that
in Jerusalem is the place where men ought to worship." Jesus said
to her, "Woman, believe Me, an hour is coming when neither in
this mountain, nor in Jerusalem, shall you worship the Father."

LORD,
there are so many churches. Which is the true church, or
where can I go to find truth I can trust? Frankly, I must
ask you this: Is God a Catholic or a Presbyterian?

God has no exclusive, local temple. The God of the local shrine ended
on the Day of Pentecost. That day the Holy Spirit made God global. Now
there are no holy lands. You must seek no special place where God is to be
found above all other places. You must not sanctify any geography or archi-
tecture as though that one place were His only dwelling place. The only
temple in which God can live for you is the temple of your own heart. Do
not seek him in any building. Only seek Him wherever there are thirsty
souls. For only there shall he be found.

Since the first century, people numbering in the millions have made
pilgrimages to see the land where I lived and taught. Many candidly are
quite disappointed, for Palestine looks a lot like the very place they live—
the place where their pilgrimage began. Where I once taught in open fields,
cities now rise, and guarded borders separate newer nations. Wars and
rumors of wars disturb the long-ago serenity that marked the land of my
birth. Therefore never make a pilgrimage to find God. You are no more or
less likely to find God in Jerusalem than in your own hometown. Every land
is holy if those who live there hunger after God.

This poor Samaritan woman was simply trying to sanctify her geography. She was saying, "Here on this particular mountain is where we say we
ought to worship. This is God's mountain." In fact she really said, "How
can you Jews say that Mount Zion is the true holy mountain, when God

clearly prefers our mountain—Mount Gerizim—as his holy mountain? Come to our mountain. Only there you will find God, right where we've built his shrine. But on your mountain—*never!*"

People are always picking out their own special mountain and calling it God's mountain. As if this is not bad enough, specific religions ever see various cities as especially central to God's will. Some call God's city Rome, some call his city Istanbul or Mecca. Make pilgrimages of any sort you like to any city that anyone has called holy. Only disappointment will come. In the end you will discover, as the woman at the well of Sychar discovered, God sometimes shows up in your own hometown, right on your block.

LORD JESUS,
I love your indwelling, never-forsaking presence.
Wherever I find need of you,
I there may bow my head and call
and find you in the only place you may be found:
my heart.

I trust my need for you finds warm supply.
My heart is shrine enough for your reply.
Amen.

34

THE CENTER OF OUR WORSHIP

JOHN 4:23-24

But an hour is coming, and now is, when the true worshipers shall worship the Father in spirit and truth; for such people the Father seeks to be His worshipers. God is a spirit, and those who worship Him must worship in spirit and truth.

LORD, declare yourself to me. I cannot touch the spiritual unless you give it flesh. Can God be God who chooses to bewilder his children by being so invisible and intangible?

How would you have received me if I had come to you as a cold idol, robed in stone or ivory?

During her Sinai existence, Israel learned that God had forbidden the worship of carved images. God allowed no artisans to create statues or paintings of what they supposed he might look like. You must hear this! God issued this second commandment to keep worshippers from imprisoning his cosmic immensity in little plaster forms. Idols do not liberate imagination. They incarcerate it in tiny, cold statues.

When artists sculpt or paint an invisible being to make it a visible image, they prevent worshippers from arriving at any conception of their own. The dimensions of God are too immense and his reality too awesome to be limited to one small, artistic conception. God is a Spirit. To try to objectify his reality is only to diminish it.

In Exodus 37 God commands Bezalel to make the ark of the covenant. He gave Bezalel exact descriptions and told him exactly how he should create the ark. Obviously, my Father is not against art. His glorious universe is testament to that. But with all of this artistic description, the mercy seat of the ark was to be left empty. This empty seat was to symbolize the earthly

71

dwelling place of God. The mercy seat appeared to be literally a seat with nobody in it.

Why?

God is a Spirit—immense, uncontainable, and indefinable. Theologians even argue that God is omni-this or omni-that. But God's immensity makes him omnicompetent. He is able to get involved in the littlest places and do the most unbelievable things.

Here then is my counsel to you: Find the wind and fire, and you will find God. But more than just finding him, you will be engulfed in his immensity. Make no pilgrimages where God once was. Seek God only where you hear he *is currently changing the world*. There you will find a revival worthy of the Spirit who summoned it. Go there! Stand in the gales. Bask in the flame! For God is a Spirit, and those who worship him must worship him in spirit and in truth.

LORD JESUS,
I love standing in my small world. For I know it is
the very middle of God's immensity.
No one can ever stand outside of God.
Not everything that is, is God.
Such an Eastern notion makes every rock and stone
the object of some pending idolatry.
Yet, Jesus, you do permeate all that is.

The Spirit bids me look and bless and see
My Maker-King in every flower and tree.
Amen.

35

THE MOST DELICIOUS FOOD OF ALL

JOHN 4:28-32

So the woman left her waterpot, and went into the city, and said to the men, "Come, see a man who told me all the things that I have done; this is not the Christ, is it?" They went out of the city and were coming to Him. In the meanwhile, the disciples were requesting Him, saying, "Rabbi, eat." But He said to them, "I have food to eat that you do not know about."

LORD,
I'm tired of filling my soul with empty, secular philosophies. I am hungry for the better food of God. Fill me, please.

You are wise to ask!

There is an exhilaration in being filled with the Spirit that surpasses every biological need and appetite. You are to be honored, for you have seen this.

Tell me what a man eats and how much and how often, and I will tell you the definition of that person. Stand by a mountain climber who has known the thin winds of towering vistas in his face, and you will know the kind of thrill that transcends common appetites. Watch some great human lover weeping for some global wound, and you will see an all-consuming appetite. Did this world-lover eat today? Did he serve any fleshly appetites? Perhaps. What we do know is that he had meat to eat that the world did not understand. Desire such meat yourself.

You must hunger for that intoxicating union with me that becomes so all consuming that it transports your spirit. Then the power of ordinary food and drink lose their hold on you.

Consider a missionary who goes to bring the Word of God to some desolate and needy place. This woman may serve alone in a small nation, a long way from the land where she received her calling. She may live through many hard times, only slowly making converts. She may even be in a great deal of danger. But she is so in love with the wonderful people she has gone to serve that her difficulties seem unimportant to her. When at last her life is spent, she is welcomed by the angels because of the appetite she served her whole life.

Do you love me? Are you possessed of a great dream? Do you have any meat to eat that the world would not understand? Pray for a consuming calling and such a Christ-filled vision that you might occasionally be completely lost in the glory of what God wants you to do. When you get that involved, you will then be so glutted with better meat that you will not mind missing the lesser meals.

LORD JESUS,
I want to eat better food than that which might
be served on plates of gold.
I want to watch a child believe.
I want to watch an old man slip from life into eternity
with a firm smile on his thin lips.
I want to see an old woman
touch her great-grandchild
with the fond light of pride shining in her old eyes.

I crave the meat that angels might applaud.
My bread shall be the entire will of God.
Amen.

36

THE HARVEST

JOHN 4:35

Do you not say, "There are yet four months, and then comes the harvest?" Behold, I say to you, lift up your eyes, and look on the fields, that they are white for harvest.

LORD, bid me to the work of harvest. Is the grain now ready for the scythe? I must ask you about the work of reaping the grain. Can I do it? I feel inadequate. The fields are large, and I am small. And gathering grain for your storage is arduous work. The fields are not sunny, they are hot. The days are long. And worst of all, the world doesn't seem to care whether or not they ever become grain for the bread of God.

The fields are white; will you serve me in the sunny harvest? You realize that evangelism has always called for an urgent harvest. How can you ever be casual about the work of reaping? Even my disciples on the day I met the woman in Samaria seemed to behave as though they were only on an outing. They had gone into town to buy provisions as though I had called them to be shoppers instead of evangelists. Then when they came back I told them that I had meat to eat that they couldn't understand (John 4:32). They seemed confused.

Compare your part in the world harvest. When the field is ready to be harvested, you must quickly set about gathering the grain, lest the driving winds or hailstorms destroy the corn. No good farmer has ever been casual about harvest. You too must see the urgency of it all.

Urgency is the issue. Tens of thousands of new churches are being started every year. Much of the globe is coming to faith. The world is turning toward me. The harvest is progressing well.

But I must ask you. Are you joyous about all those who are coming to faith? Are you delighted that each hour you have thousands of new brothers and sisters of many colors and languages around the world? Does it not

thrill you that these precious ones are finding a more meaningful definition of life?

I pray you, help me with my harvest. Lift up your eyes. I am the hope
of this hopeless world. Care about it, for only if you do can you really
understand the heart of God. Love all whom I love. Come, we shall love
them together.

LORD JESUS,
I know God's heart is broken
over all of those who are lost.
But my heart is broken because I have
so little concern about what God cares most about.
Help me to feel the lostness
of the world and to see
God weeping over fields white for harvest.

I would be like you Lord, so let me reap
and cry about those things that make God weep.
Amen.

37

SHOW BUSINESS
AND HUMAN NEED

JOHN 4:46-48

He came therefore again to Cana of Galilee where He had made the water wine. And there was a certain royal official, whose son was sick at Capernaum. When he heard that Jesus had come out of Judea into Galilee, he went to Him, and was requesting Him to come down and heal his son; for he was at the point of death. Jesus therefore said to him, "Unless you people see signs and wonders, you simply will not believe."

LORD,
the world is a weeping place. Yet so often the church seems to be more of a theater than a hospital. Entertainment has replaced ministry. I see so many in need of splints and bandages, and our triage is flawed. They bleed and die while we're dispensing song and dance.

You must understand my rebuke was not to the poor man whose son was at the point of death. I was back in Cana where I had all too recently made wine from water. I sensed that the poor man's need to save his dying son had put a glint of hope in the eye of these of Cana who would see a miracle. They were still abuzz about the wine miracle, and now they thought they were in for another miraculous sign.

It was here that my heart was most torn. I knew the man was in desperate straits, and yet I had not the slightest desire to offer miracles on demand to gratify those people who wanted me to be some kind of glitzy faith healer in the business of religious entertainment. So I said to them frankly, "Unless you people see signs and wonders, you simply will not believe" (John 4:48).

You have a taste for compassion, but you must also realize how religious miracles are easily subverted to entertainment. You have seen that show-biz is always a temptation in the church. Some churches have honestly gotten into this show-biz gospel in the attempt to exorcise the demons of congregational boredom from their worship. Then they move from the Spirit's direction to hype. Few of these mean to adopt hype and abandon the Spirit. But in trying to keep things exciting and positive, they trade worship for glitz.

Let me suggest that the only foolproof way you can know that I am present in worship is to ask a more difficult question: Is the Lord present in the worship leader? Worship leaders void of me can become quite proficient at entertainment, but they cannot lead in real adoration. Your need is therefore rooted in their integrity.

Your salvation is an issue of simple worship; your worship will require you to walk and talk with me. This is your best hope of honest adoration.

I call you to an honest hope. Pursue me. Love me. Adore me in the quiet places of your heart. Then those sign-mongers who want to make the church a religious show will be amazed. Worship, and as you pray you will never try to fill your need with glitz. When you seek the love of God in the silent center of your life, you will always find your adoration exhilarating and substantial.

LORD JESUS,
I am needy, and I know
all those with whom I worship are needy too.
Would you come to us
and teach us true soul hunger so that
we never can be satisfied with any smaller definition
of worship than that
which starts and ends with you alone?

Help me to turn from glitzy praise and start
to meet you at the altar of my heart.
Amen.

38

THE GREATER MIRACLES GROW FROM THE LESSER

JOHN 4:49-54

The royal official said to Him, "Sir, come down before my child dies." Jesus said to him, "Go your way, your son lives." The man believed the word that Jesus spoke to him, and he started off. And as he was now going down, his slaves met him, saying that his son was living. So he inquired of them the hour when he began to get better. They said therefore to him, "Yesterday at the seventh hour the fever left him." So the father knew that it was at that hour in which Jesus said to him, "Your son lives"; and he himself believed, and his whole household. This is again a second sign that Jesus performed, when He had come out of Judea into Galilee.

LORD,
I have needs so great that only a miracle can heal them.

Great! Miracles are my specialty.

A certain Roman official had a son who was dying. He was so near death that he lived with only that narrow definition of life that is defined by respiration and heartbeat. It was because he was so near death that his entire family came to receive that life that far transcends mere breath and pulse. The greatest miracle was not that their son came out of a coma. The greatest miracle is that the entire family came to receive imperishable life and immortality.

Be careful in this world, lest you celebrate the wrong miracles. The possibility of this grave error is hidden in every public healing service. God's glory can be lost in flashy religious exhibitions that make it possible for the lesser truths to eclipse the greater. Do not spend your lives chasing after faith healers. They sometimes do rather remarkable things, but in offering temporary life, they often downplay the greatest miracle of all, eternal life.

Do you not see it! To be born again is not a mere transaction between you and God. When anyone is born again, a genuine miracle occurs.

Human destiny changes. Life escapes its narrow "pulse and breath" definition. Suddenly those who experience my love come to know grace. Your own circumstances, however desperate, can then take on a kind of holy common sense. The tangled circumstances of your life are called to untangle themselves because you love God. For even those who are healed of terminal afflictions must face death again sooner or later. But those who know this miracle will never die.

So the official's son was healed and he lived—for a while. He lived longer than he would have lived if I had not healed him. But don't miss the central miracle of that day. The father believed. His entire house was saved. That boy is now in heaven forever and will bear you testimony that on the day I healed him, he received two kinds of life—the smaller biological kind and the enduring, eternal kind. He later forfeited the first kind. He continues enjoying the second.

LORD JESUS,
I too much treasure
treasures that are not.

Help me to see that miracles of faith
are substance of your sacrificial grace.
Amen.

39

THE MAIN THING

LUKE 4:16-21

And He came to Nazareth, where He had been brought up; and as was His custom, He entered the synagogue on the Sabbath, and stood up to read. And the book of the prophet Isaiah was handed to Him. And He opened the book, and found the place where it was written,

> The spirit of the Lord is upon Me,
> Because He has anointed Me to preach the gospel to the poor.
> He has sent Me to proclaim release to the captives,
> And recovery of sight to the blind,
> To set free those who are downtrodden,
> To proclaim the favorable year of the Lord.

And He closed the book, and gave it back to the attendant, and sat down; and the eyes of all in the synagogue were fixed upon Him. And He began to say to them, "Today this Scripture has been fulfilled in your hearing."

LORD, am I called to do what you came to do? Are we in the same business? And even if I am, it sure is hard to preach your reality in this place, for I am very well-known here.

It is hard to appear interested in the work of God where we are best known. I preached my first hometown sermon among my relatives and acquaintances. In that sermon I said I had come to preach good news to the poor, set the prisoners free, heal the blind, and announce the arrival of God's kingdom. The text of my sermon was taken from Isaiah. These ancient words—they were ancient even when I preached on them—are now the charter of my church. The qualities of the Spirit that Isaiah named are still the key issues of servanthood that define what a church ought to be.

These things described my ministry too. I came to preach the good news to the poor. The poor in any age rarely get any good news. But in me they got it. They, the destitute, the hungry, and the powerless opened the gospel gift to discover that God had written them into his will. They discovered they were the inheritors of great wealth. This was good news indeed!

My Father sent me to tell the prisoners that their release had been secured. Besides giving the poor an inheritance, I came to liberate prisoners. My life to them was like receiving a letter of pardon from the governor. These prisoners of a harsh life walked out of their stone walls and iron bars. Their confining gates swung open to the fresh new air of morning. Their gloomy dungeons gave way to the outside—to songbirds and sunlight.

And the blind, whose every step was taken in darkness…what of them? What of those who had never seen the food they ate or the lovely faces of the children that they had brought into their dark world? Now all is changed! The blind can see!

But the best part of my work was to proclaim the current moment as the year of God's grace. Think of this glorious announcement! No one ever has to wait for the coming of God's grace. It is here and now. Nobody has to work hard, study hard, and wonder if someday God will smile down on them and decide to give them grace. He is giving it even now. This is the acceptable year of the Lord! This current year!

Isaiah's glorious definition of what I came to do is exactly what you must finish up for me. I did it while I was on earth, and now I have committed it unto you.

LORD JESUS,
I want to finish what you began.
I am your feet; lead me where you want me to walk.
I am your hands; show me what you want me to do.
I want to preach the gospel,
liberate captives,
give the blind their sight,
and tell everyone that now is the day
they may be saved.
In short,

this is your work to which my call must cling,
and keep this gold of yours as one true thing.
Amen.

40

PHYSICIAN, HEAL YOURSELF!

LUKE 4:22-24
And all were speaking well of Him, and wondering at the gracious
words which were falling from His lips; and they were saying, "Is
this not Joseph's son?" And He said to them, "No doubt you will
quote this proverb to Me, 'Physician, heal yourself! Whatever we
heard was done in Capernaum, do here in your home town as
well.'"
And He said, "Truly I say to you, no prophet is welcome in his
home town."

LORD,
I wish my reputation were more noble. It's not that it is
ignoble, it's just that it is largely absent. It's hard to think
well of myself when most people never think of me at
all.

I've known the scourge of low reputation. Early in my ministry my
enemies began to cry that I was mentally ill. It was a slur of grand propor-
tions to lay on me. I had healed others by common report, but I was called
a healer who could not deal with his own mental illness.

My hometown people had watched me grow up, and they thought they
knew me. You suffer from the same kind of low community respect. The
people of Nazareth saw their knowledge of me as a kind of containment.
Your acquaintances too may have limited your world by what they think
they know of it. My hometown acquaintances knew me only in a surface
way, a shallow way that kept them from receiving me in any other way. So
it may be with those in your world. This is familiarity's worst sin: Once you
let your world define you in small ways, it will never be free to know you
by any larger definition.

There are two kinds of repentance. First you must feel bad about ordinary moral transgressions. Then you must master intellectual repentance.
Intellectual repentance is your failure to admit that your ideas need an over-
haul.

The Nazarenes in my hometown committed the second kind of sin and needed the second kind of repentance. They stamped their feet and said, "We know Jesus to be thus and so, and we refuse to know him in any other way." You see, pride is the real barrier to intellectual repentance. You don't like publicly admitting you are wrong. Nobody does. But you must not go on being wrong only to keep from confessing you are wrong.

Peter sinned the sins of these Nazarenes at my trial. When first asked if he was an acquaintance of mine, he lied and said no. Then, of course, he couldn't change his mind without looking wishy-washy. So he continued denying me rather than risk looking bad in front of the group.

You are feeling a bit of pain I learned that day in Nazareth. I hated to hear them scream their errors loudly and collectively. I knew they would later have a hard time changing their minds. They never did—at least most of them. So remember that because we are partners in the kingdom, you will know some of what I knew and feel something of what I felt. But there is a point to it all: You the servant and I the Lord are in the same great business of making victory rise from tombs.

LORD JESUS,
help me confess where my loud affirmations
have proven wrong.
Help me confess that arrogance
that damns all those who will not change
their minds
and thus are powerless to change their destinations.

I'm sorry, Lord, that even when I've lied,
I find it hard repenting of my pride.
Amen.

41

STAYING IN CHARGE
OF YOUR EMOTIONS

LUKE 4:28-30
And all in the synagogue were filled with rage as they heard these
things; and they rose up and cast Him out of the city, and led Him
to the brow of the hill on which their city had been built, in order
to throw Him down the cliff. But passing through their midst, He
went His way.

LORD,
I sometimes allow my anger too much leeway. How can
I have control of my emotions at all times?

The worst thing about letting your anger take control is that the
moment you do it, you are no longer in control. Further, when you lose
control, you often vent your anger on your closest family and friends. In the
Nazarene synagogue, the people I knew best were the ones who became
enraged enough to think of killing me. They tried to kill me, not in the
"legal" way that Pilate and the midnight mob later used, but in an incensed
and murderous outrage in which their anger took charge.

The entire Nazarene community was enraged, including our small-town
patriarchs—Jacob, Abraham, and Isaac—as well as Nazareth's elite—her
bootmakers, carpenters, wine vendors, and meat merchants. These were the
very people who had befriended me all through my synagogue years. They
had been at my bar mitzvah. Yet in a fit of rage they rushed upon me and
in violence pushed me out of the synagogue. At the edge of town they tried
to push me over the edge of the precipice. Ordinarily I loved those bluffs.
I had played along those cliffs in my childhood.

Living within your own community can be good. But remember this:
Communities, warm as they are, do not always afford you a good place to
grow intellectually or stretch your mind with new ideas. Great truths are
rarely discovered in small towns. That's because small communities derive
their warmth from everyone's desire never to be controversial with each

other. Communities gain their never-changing hometown appeal by never changing their ideas. They do not become warm communities by practicing any real openness to new ideas.

I say all this to remind you that change comes slow in comfortable communities. And the number one reaction to change is anger. So love your community while you welcome dissent. Show yourself tolerant; you may someday need the tolerance of others. But above all, learn self-control.

In Nazareth that day, I was almost killed not for thinking up a new truth but for preaching Isaiah, a very old truth they knew quite well. I didn't change a thing they knew about the passage. Yet I was nearly martyred by people who lost control of their anger. So live in peace. Stay in charge of your emotions. It is the only way you will ever learn to live without regret.

LORD JESUS,
I know you are the Way, the Truth, and the Life.
You were the Way of courage,
the Truth unafraid, and
the Life of utter integrity.
And best of all, you never lost control of your emotions.

Please help me stay in charge of all I feel.
Make self-control my drink, my bread, my meal.
Amen.

42

IMMEDIATELY

MATTHEW 4:18-20
And walking by the Sea of Galilee, He saw two brothers, Simon
who was called Peter, and Andrew his brother, casting a net into
the sea; for they were fishermen. And He said to them, "Follow
Me, and I will make you fishers of men." And they immediately
left the nets, and followed Him.

LORD,
I want to follow you...but tomorrow. I want to learn to
pray...but tomorrow. Shouldn't I think through things
before I begin jumping to decisions that could hurt me?
Help me know when I should take a leap of faith and
when I should think things through. Help me to distinguish between making good, slow decisions and
cowardly procrastinations.

Never be overly impulsive, but remember that God's holiest adverb is
immediately. Immediately is the word that describes when and how God
wants you to obey him.

Remember my marvelous pun, my humorous and terrifying double
truth, "Follow me, and I will make you fishers of men." This fishing business is your business too. My earliest disciples were fishers, a noble occupation but one that was far beneath all that God had in mind for them.
How could they know the cosmic reasons for which ordinary fishing would
lose its hold on their lives? But do not stand in awe at their vocation. Their
calling is yours.

The apostles were signing on to become an international team of public
speakers and gospel writers. They had always believed they would live and
die in the comfortable circle of their small Capernaum society. They
thought they would die and be buried after a lifetime of mending soggy
nets and hawking their wares in the streets. But their worst fault is that they
had grown accustomed to life in the slow lane. They had no grand dreams.

They believed they would die rehearsing those Old Testament truths that forged their narrow, safe communities.

Old Testament was an unknown term then, but in time they themselves would create the term by writing the New Testament. They could not know all this, for my Father delivers his heaviest, unbearable truths in bite-size precepts. That day all they needed to understand were two words: *Follow me.* And they did follow—*immediately.* From their little Galilee, they would follow me into bloody arenas and hostile, pagan cultures.

I called Peter to be my disciple on that long-ago day. His "follow me" ultimately led to Rome itself. There can be no doubt that Peter died a long way from Galilee. And the one reason that he marked this world in ways that eluded all his understanding was that he knew the never-look-back glory of God's holiest adverb, *immediately.*

The one key issue for you lies in the readiness with which you follow me in the present moment. Your eternal greatness is hidden in your ability to obey God quickly in the present moment. You have only to claim God's adverb. All you have to pray is this: "God, call me to do whatever you will. Disclose as much or as little of your plan as you will. You will find me ready to follow you wherever you ask. I'll go—*immediately.*"

LORD JESUS,
now is when I need to know what you want.
Immediately *is the time frame in which I must obey you.*
Yes, I am as busy as a fisherman at his nets,
but no matter,
the worth of my discipleship has always been
my open and immediate response to your interruptions of my life.

So here I yield; come call me, and you'll see
that I'll do all of it immediately.
Amen.

43

THE OBLIGATION
OF HEALING

MARK 1:29-31
And immediately after they had come out of the synagogue, they
came into the house of Simon and Andrew, with James and John.
Now Simon's mother-in-law was lying sick with a fever; and immediately they spoke to Him about her. And He came to her and
raised her up, taking her by the hand, and the fever left her, and
she waited on them.

LORD,
grace is what I receive from you. Yet how shall I give it
back? You taught me long ago that grace never stays fresh
with the keeping. To grasp at it is to be a physician who
will not care about the contagion gathered all around
him. How soon after I am saved should I begin to serve?

Keep nothing sweet too long, lest it sour. Give away what you have
received. To accept any gift from God is to accept the obligation of that gift.
Once I visited Peter's home, only to find his mother-in-law at the brink of
death. I could see in Peter's eyes that masculine glint that will not submit
to open tears. It was easy to see he loved his mother-in-law. There was only
one thing to be done—love named the miracle. Peter's mother-in-law was
healed of a critical fever. But it was what she did next that was so beautiful. She got up and served those who were guests in her house. She had
received the gift of healing, and she understood that to be well again obligated her to serve others.

She knew what you know—the word *grace* means "gift," but it is not a
gift to be grasped but one to be shared.

Grace has a double meaning. A ballerina has gifts. So does a sculptor.
There are two kinds of gifts: those that are ornaments and those designed
to be used. There are "art" gifts and "tool" gifts. God gives both kinds. God
is an artist and gives freely all those gifts whose design is to make the world

more beautiful. But the best grace—gifts of the Spirit—are those gifts that are designed to be used in ministry.

As I called my disciples to be servants, I have also called you to serve. When you have served me, your service will be your gift. Your obedience will at last become the ornament that makes my saving grace a gilded and beautiful thing in the lives of others.

When you are most mature, you will ask at every moment of your walk with me, "Lord, my hands are now free from my last assignment. Tell me, what is my next?"

In the end your service will be an object of beauty. Angels will stand hushed by your obedience. The word *Lord* will be the chief ornament of your service. Come follow me and join yourself to those who carry basins and towels and stoop to wash the feet of the proud who have never known the joy of your calling. Ask all who live in need of me, "I have been healed by the Savior; what can I do for you?"

You have received my gifts in abundance. Now give as you have received.

LORD JESUS,
I have looked and lived.
I have received your gift of life.
I have looked upon your cross and marveled
that you paid so great a price for me.
I have been healed by your
unceasing miracles in my life.

I ask you, now that I have been made new,
"What is it, Lord, you have for me to do?"
Amen.

44

LESSONS ON SILENCING LOUD-MOUTHED DEMONS

And when evening had come, after the sun had set, they began bringing to Him all who were ill and those who were demon-possessed. And the whole city had gathered at the door. And He healed many who were ill with various diseases, and cast out many demons; and He was not permitting the demons to speak, because they knew who He was.

LORD,
I've never doubted the reality of Satan. I spend too much time fighting him to question his reality. Help me to reply to all his allurements with a powerful *no*. I need to rebuff his temptations with strength even when I feel like I'm losing. Can he be beaten? Every time?

In my earthly sojourn, I was ever torn between the poles of a splendid paradox. I was eager to tell the world I was God's Son. But I also knew that this eager disclosure must reckon with the critical issue of timing. So I often deferred the joy of revealing my identity so I would not hasten my inevitable crucifixion. I knew if I became too open, those terminal cries of "crucify!" would come too soon. I would then cut short the time I needed to instruct my followers.

But my Enemy knew who I was. So when I cast out demons, I would often forbid them to tell what they knew about me. They were eager, of course, to thwart the purposes of God by pushing me toward a premature declaration of my messiahship and death.

Never be amazed that demons obey me. You, through me, are equally their master. They will yield to my name. They always have, and they always will. If they could disobey the demand of God, they would be as powerful as God. Christianity degenerates to superstition when it accords Satan such power.

You are a receptacle of grace, and grace is all-powerful. You must never allow yourself to see the supernatural world as a kind of dualism. Dualism is that false doctrine that teaches that the world is the battleground of a black god named Satan and a white god named Jehovah. How false! For you there are not two gods, there is only one. Satan is not your god, nor does he have any of my power. He cannot threaten you. He has already been judged and is awaiting his final sentence. He can do you no harm.

Remember, as demons were once subject to my power, they are now equally subject to my power in your life. Satan is as subject to me in your age as he was in my own. In my name he must obey you. He has no choice in the matter. He does have great power in relation to you but not to me. If you would order him out of your affairs, command him in my name.

Just as Satan tried to hurry me into a premature disclosure of God's will, he will try to hurry you as well. He will glory in the mistakes you will make when he has tricked you into forgetting that you are my child and that you are meant to dwell confidently in my favor. If he can manage to do that, you will be his, and he will sift you as wheat for his own purposes. Therefore never give him any entrance to your life. Your heart does not have enough room for both me and him. Just speak my name in his presence. That is all. He will be silent. You will be free.

LORD JESUS,
I want nothing more than
to understand
that Satan is my Enemy,
conquered already by the cross.
I claim that power at every moment when
he seeks to make me afraid.

I exorcise these foes who bar my way;
I know the name whose force they must obey.
Amen.

45

A FRIGHTENING ABUNDANCE

LUKE 5:1-8

Now it came about that while the multitude were pressing around Him and listening to the Word of God, He was standing by the lake of Gennesaret; and He saw two boats lying at the edge of the lake; but the fishermen had gotten out of them, and were washing their nets. And He got into one of the boats, which was Simon's, and asked him to put out a little way from the land. And He sat down and began teaching the multitudes from the boat. And when He had finished speaking, He said to Simon, "Put out into the deep water and let down your nets for a catch."

And Simon answered and said, "Master, we worked hard all night and caught nothing, but at Your bidding I will let down the nets." And when they had done this, they enclosed a great quantity of fish; and their nets began to break; and they signaled to their partners in the other boat, for them to come and help them. And they came, and filled both of the boats, so that they began to sink. But when Simon Peter saw that, he fell down at Jesus' feet, saying, "Depart from me, for I am a sinful man, O Lord!"

LORD, we are all frightened by the prospect of having too little to give. Poverty is a need that always lies beneath our spoken fears. But I am often stopped not by my poverty but by my riches in Christ, by your lavish abundance. You give so freely, so richly. I am overwhelmed by the sheer volume of your treasure.

The overwhelming power of my godhood may sometimes surprise you as it did Peter one day. He wanted fish, but when he found himself buried in them, he was suddenly frightened by the sheer size of grace. Seeing the unbelievable happen before your very eyes can send chills down your spine. The terror caused Peter to shrink back from God's rich supply.

Sometimes God gives you so much, so all at once, it can terrify you.

My ministry was and always will be an encounter with the unbeliev-able. The day I called, "Lazarus, come forth!" was like that. The day I stopped the funeral procession in Nain and ordered the young man out of his coffin was also such a day. The day I touched the ten lepers and all of their eroded flesh became new before the wide eyes of the staring crowd was such a day.

Grace baffles those unused to its volume.

But for you, I beg you, accept my extravagance and remember that the more things seem explainable, the less I am involved. I feel sorry for those church members who settle for half a life in my abundance, those who are doing good things but whose lives are quite explainable in human terms. Most of them at the first of their Christian experience knew me well. Miracles were then as customary as prayer. Then somewhere along the way the extraordinary became the customary. In time they trained themselves to be content with rigid routines. The electrifying miracles that had first drawn them to me were replaced by all things canned and customary. Sadly, they are now at a loss to tell you when the vital Christ they first knew was replaced by small religious habits.

Are you at a loss to recall the last time you saw something so wonder-ful in your life that I was the only possible explanation of it all?

Please, will you come back to me? End the feeling that you are working hard but achieving nothing? Escape the milieu of these weary, productless apostles? End the feeling that you have fished all night and caught nothing? Take the advice I gave to Peter. Cast out your nets in a better name, and your life will become productive again. Will I indwell your life so that your empty fishing can be replaced by the power of all I supply?

LORD JESUS,
I am trapped in mundane churchmanship.
I can't remember when, like Peter,
I fell down before your overwhelming power,
amazed at anything out of the ordinary in my church.
I am too captive to the mundane and the explainable.
Please forgive me.

Grace rains in joy, displacing all the bland
with life too wonderful to understand.
Amen.

46

SIN AND DISEASE

LUKE 5:17-20

And it came about one day that He was teaching; and there were some Pharisees and teachers of the law sitting there, who had come from every village of Galilee and Judea and from Jerusalem; and the power of the Lord was present for Him to perform healing. And behold, some men were carrying on a bed a man who was paralyzed; and they were trying to bring him in, and to set him down in front of Him. And not finding any way to bring him in because of the crowd, they went up on the roof and let him down through the tiles with his stretcher, right in the center, in front of Jesus. And seeing their faith, He said, "Friend, your sins are forgiven you."

LORD,
I don't feel good when I must pray with folded, dirty hands. Help me to see that the state of my heart and the abundance of your forgiveness are but two sides of the same page. You spent lavishly to cleanse me. I sin when I choose to live with guilt.

You have come to see a splendid truth. My forgiveness has made you well.

You understand that suffering is connected with guilt. Many who suffer an illness cannot see what you have seen.

My own countrymen who saw me daily performing miracles often saw no relationship between their physical diseases and their sin. This paralytic provided me an opportunity to remind them of the real truth. Do you see the plaintive picture? The house was full. The doorways jammed. We were talking about the various in and outs of Jewish theology. Then came this paralyzed man who could not afford theology as a discussion. He was too needy. He could not walk. He had to depend upon friends to carry him to me. They did, but when he arrived he found a heavy discussion in progress. The theology was thick.

The paralytic was desperate.

His friends, at his encouragement, took the tiles from the roof of the house and lowered him through the ceiling. Soon he was lying directly before me. I forgave his sins. He did not ask me to do it, and the religious leaders were agog that I claimed to be able to do it.

Please remember that my forgiveness and your healing go together. The reason many people are sick is that they languish under heavy guilt that has either created their suffering or contributed to it. In the case of this paralytic, it was definitely so. I could have either forgiven his sin or told him to rise and walk. I dealt first with his sin. Even if I gave him back his legs and left his heart full of guilt, he would never have been really well.

Have you learned the secret of power that comes from a clean heart? Paralyzed legs are not as big an issue with God as a paralyzed heart.

Are you prevented from full joy because you carry some unforgiven sin? Sort out the cause of your paralysis. Is there some grudge you have never been able to forgive? Come to me. Give up your sins, and I will clothe you with a lightness of being. You will then know the joy of our open friendship unhindered by any barriers. I will cry, "You are fully mine," and you will reply, "Forever."

LORD JESUS,
I am so often a spiritual paralytic.
I can't move freely in my world to win others
because I am too much paralyzed by the very sins
I would like to heal in others.
Please, I beg you,

cleanse my sins, and when the cleaning's done,
teach my legless soul to serve and run.
Amen.

SPIRITUAL NEED AND RELIGIOUS COMFORT

LUKE 5:29-32
And Levi gave a big reception for Him in his house; and there was a great crowd of tax-gatherers and other people who were reclining at the table with them. And the Pharisees and their scribes began grumbling at His disciples, saying, "Why do you eat and drink with the tax-gatherers and sinners?" And Jesus answered and said to them, "It is not those who are well who need a physician, but those who are sick. I have not come to call the righteous but sinners to repentance."

LORD,
I often catch myself feeling like I really belong in church. Everybody there seems almost sinless in light of their immaculate appearance. I feel good just being among the people who are righteous. You just feel good about yourself when you're with the right people.

Be careful. The Pharisees sinned by feeling good that they had become so much like God. Your own self-esteem may actively be in the way of really getting to know God. People who feel too good about who they are at church may have already traded religiosity for spirituality. Never get your spirituality and religiosity confused. There's quite a difference. In fact, religiosity is usually in the way of spirituality.

The Pharisees in Levi's house were religious. They religiously kept their times of worship and their notes on sermons and lectures. But Levi and his group of tax-gathering associates needed God, not religion. Churchmanship can end up in that strict kind of religiosity that loves theology but doesn't care much for God. Spirituality, on the other hand, is born in ardor, and ardor is that passion of spirit that cries out its need and wildly celebrates God's presence in the life. Here is the checklist that will help you know whether you're spiritual or religious.

First, do you feel worse when you realize you're sitting in church with a spot on your suit than you do when you've passed over an opportunity to help someone in need?

Second, are you faster to criticize the choir for hitting a few sour notes than you are to judge your own religious contentment?

Third, which makes you more angry, being overlooked for a position on the church financial board or your church's failure to minister in the inner city?

Finally, when you list the things you most like about church, do you start out by listing the church bowling club or its missionary conscience?

The Pharisees at Levi's house loved talking theology but rarely made friends of those people who couldn't. They knew the book of Leviticus backward, but they rarely stopped and talked to the poor.

This tax-gatherer, Levi, would ultimately write one of the books of the New Testament. Would he have written it if I had met him with stern religiosity instead of warm spirituality? I think not.

In me, the tax-gatherers had a rabbi who met them Spirit-first. You too have such a teacher. But do the real riches of your life emanate from your habitual religious practice, or do they come from your reliance on the Spirit? Lay by your proud religiosity. Meet me Spirit-first.

LORD JESUS,
rules are as easy as learning to read manuals,
but spirituality comes only from the disciplines of prayer
and Bible reading.
The Pharisees thought that they were doing the excellent work
of studying the Scripture,
but it was the work of the Spirit by which you made
friends of the outcasts.

I want to let your life flow out of me,
free of dead religiosity.
Amen.

48
—

THE OBLIGATION OF JOY

MARK 2:18-20

And John's disciples and the Pharisees were fasting; and they came
and said to Him, "Why do John's disciples and the disciples of the
Pharisees fast, but Your disciples do not fast?"

And Jesus said to them, "While the bridegroom is with them,
the attendants of the bridegroom do not fast, do they? So long as
they have the bridegroom with them, they cannot fast. But the days
will come when the bridegroom is taken away from them, and then
they will fast in that day."

LORD,
praise is one of the life signs of the church. It is definitely a life sign in matters of my own personal faith. A
faith that will not revel in joy is just a grumpy allegiance
and no faith at all. But tell me, Jesus, how can I be sure
I am a person of joy? How can I keep my faith singing?

It's a simple matter of remembering that joy is your response to our
togetherness.

The disciples of John the Baptist and the Pharisees were both marked
with one commonality in their mystique: They were too serious. The
Pharisees were especially stern with their religion. They weren't above
laughter, but they had to have a very good reason to do it. Their laughter
was so infrequent that if you saw a Pharisee doubled over in laughter, you
marked the day and hour. The Pharisees were stern because the law was
stern. The Pharisees served a stern God. This God from time to time
shouted down over the balustrades of heaven, "Are you having a good
time?"

If ever a Pharisee felt inclined to answer, "Yes, God, we are!" God would
shout back, "Well, stop it! Are you religious leaders or not?"

John the Baptist's disciples were also very serious. John was a fiery
preacher whose sermons focused on the coming apocalypse.

To them, laughter was frivolous because the time was short. Many of

99

John's disciples and most of the Pharisee's disciples did not appreciate the fact that I went to parties. I liked parties. I loved life. I enjoyed my disciples, and they enjoyed me. We walked, it seemed, along a million miles of dusty roads, talking and laughing as we went. The fellowship I enjoyed with those men was glorious. In the warmth of our manhood we had so much life to enjoy. We laughed as we drank wine and devoured good food. We did this so much that those who laughed less called us partygoers—gluttons and winebibbers.

Let your joy also come from our togetherness. You are mine, and I am yours. Give me some hallelujah to mark our friendship. We are one!

One of the martyrs would later say—in spite of burning stakes and savage beasts—"Joy really is the most infallible proof of the presence of God." The apostle Paul thought so too. He once wrote that we ought always to be joyful.

Express your joy either because you feel it or because you eagerly anticipate it. Practice joy until you do feel it, or let it burst forth because it is honestly there. It is not false to fake joy if you are really seeking it. It is only false to fake it to connote the impression of some victory you do not own. Practice joy, therefore, either because you seek it or because you already own it.

LORD JESUS,
I am here, and you are here.
You cannot fail regardless,
and I cannot fail when you are
the welcome occupant of the throne of my heart.

Bring on the dance and let the anthems raise,
for joy demands that I erupt in praise.
Amen.

49

NEW WINE

No one sews a patch of unshrunk cloth on an old garment; otherwise the patch pulls away from it, the new from the old, and a worse tear results. And no one puts new wine into old wineskins; otherwise the wine will burst the skins, and the wine is lost, and the skins as well; but one puts new wine into fresh wineskins.

LORD,
when is tradition a bad thing?

When it leaves you satisfied with boring anthems and dead orthodoxy. You are the reason I came to make all things new, just as you yourself have been made new. I don't want you ever to see Christianity as retailored Judaism. For you, I have made the world new and provided a faith that I intend to be new every morning.

In this striking metaphor of new wine, I want you to know that my new faith was like new wine—too tart and delicious for old wineskins. It's all about what you want—the dull traditions of old things or the excitement and vitality of new things. I had no intention of trying to take the rich, pure grace of the Christian faith and "Judaize" it with the Haggadah, the Torah, or any of the customary traditions. Those traditions were beautiful. They were strong. They had kept Judaism intact for thousands of years. But in me, God was beginning something brand-new. Christianity is not a faith made up from the scraps of other dull religious habits, the leftover parts of something lost and long gone.

Christianity is new wine! Heady new wine! With this wine I want to fill you strong enough to intoxicate your dreams. I want you to taste and see that God is good and that I make all things new.

Let this wine, so warm and heady, draw you ever closer to a world of final and grand communion. This wine must reach you with grace as a drink to strengthen and refresh you. May it keep you ever thirsty for everlasting truth.

This wine is the wine of the New Covenant. It is intoxicating and expansive. It will let you dream again, and can be had for merely crying, "I believe." This wine is the glory of heaven. Drink of this salvation and then turn and offer your cup to all.

LORD JESUS,
I have tasted your new wine,
and my mind is drunk with a new delirium.
I am heady with the inebriation
that God was in Christ, reconciling.

Come, wine, addict me to your blest employ.
Inebriate me with narcotic joy.
Amen.

50

OUTRUNNING THE ANGELS

JOHN 5:1-5

After these things there was a feast of the Jews, and Jesus went up to Jerusalem. Now there is in Jerusalem by the sheep gate a pool, which is called in Hebrew Bethesda, having five porticoes. In these lay a multitude of those who were sick, blind, lame, and withered, [waiting for the moving of the waters; for an angel of the Lord went down at certain seasons into the pool, and stirred up the water; whoever then first, after the stirring up of the water, stepped in was made well from whatever disease with which he was afflicted]. And a certain man was there, who had been thirty-eight years in his sickness.

LORD,
there are a few people I wish I liked better. There are circumstances in life I wish I could change. I find that those with poor character and poor values disgust me. Politicians have a way of raising a throbbing, dull dislike within me. What am I to do?

Beware a constant dislike of anyone or any set of circumstances, for if you nurse your dislikes, they degenerate first to bitterness and then to grudges. Beware that your unfulfilled hopes don't lead you to become bitter toward those who seem to live life better than you do.

Let me give you a glimpse of counterfeit hope. I met a poor man who came day after day to five porches to wait on the descent of an angel into a pool. According to popular lore, whoever first entered the pool right after the angel came would be healed of whatever sickness he had.

How pitiful are the doctrines of the damned. How foolish are their hopes. Here at Bethesda was an odd and tedious superstition. This man had waited for 38 years for his sluggard angel to show up. As you can imagine, in four decades he had developed quite a grudge against his tardy angel.

There is a kind of bitterness that comes from watching angels bless everyone but ourselves. The blessings of others can make us angry at God.

Then bit by bit our anger turns to grudges against the Almighty. Be careful, for nothing is so everlastingly destructive as bitterness. It grows into a complex and sour entanglement. It wraps its sniveling tentacles around all largesse of spirit.

Bitterness is the grudge of Esau, lying in wait to get even. Bitterness occupied the heart of Judas. Bitterness eats the souls of congregational factions whose unforgiveness destroys the church. One of the New Testament writers reminds us, "Make every effort to live in peace with all men and to be holy; without holiness no one will see the Lord. See to it that no one misses the grace of God, and that no bitter root grows up to cause trouble and defile many" (Hebrews 12:14-15 NIV).

Do you see the image of this "root of bitterness"? If so, see that it never owns you. The writer of Hebrews is really saying that roots of bitterness, like the roots of a tree, thread their way into the soil and intertwine with other roots. Look at a great tree in the distance. Let its forking and leafy branches remind you that their complexity above ground suggests another system of branches equally complex growing under the earth. It is not possible to pull such a root system out of the ground without destroying all the earth around the tree. Therefore permit no bitterness to grow in your heart, lest you one day have to tear its roots from your life. In tearing them out you may destroy great relationships and damage a thousand interconnected friendships.

Do not be like this man who waited 38 years on a sluggish angel. Above all, never let your bitterness destroy your relationships. Learn to bless others who have met the healing angel you never found. Learn to rejoice when grace passes close enough for you to see it but doesn't touch you. Then you will find my sufficiency so great that you will wonder that you ever thought you needed either grudges or angels.

LORD JESUS,
I must confess, I too have often waited on sluggish angels,
trying to get ahead of the greedier and healthier.
I grew angry and sullied my heart because
someone else always seemed to beat me to the blessings of God.
Forgive me for such selfish spirituality.

I shun the tardy angels in life's pond,
and hunger for the waiting Christ beyond.
Amen.

51

DO YOU WANT TO GET WELL?

JOHN 5:6-9

When Jesus saw him lying there, and knew that he had already been a long time in that condition, He said to him, "Do you wish to get well?"

The sick man answered Him, "Sir, I have no man to put me in the pool when the water is stirred up, but while I am coming, another steps down before me."

Jesus said to him, "Arise, take up your pallet, and walk."

And immediately the man became well, and took up his pallet and began to walk.

LORD,
I like being the center of attention. I like being fussed over. I don't really like being sick, but I sure like to have everyone say, "Now, now, my friend, I'll be thinking about you." I love for people to think about me. Am I sick? I mean, really sick?

It is not wrong to enjoy being the center of attention, but it is wrong to need to be.

Somehow you remind me of the man who couldn't outrun his angel.

My question to him was this: After 38 years of being sick, did he really want to quit being the center of attention? All those who carried him to the pool each day were under his command. His sickness became his way to wield power over others. Was there no one to put him in the water after it was stirred? Why not? It was likely because those who had carried him there had tired of his endless complaints. His self-pity had likely come to result in a whimpering life: "Alas, poor me, I have none to put me in the pool." His friends might secretly have desired to have put him in the pool and left him there. Self-pity usually frightens away all those who find little joy in consoling whining hypochondriacs.

Conversations with Jesus

Sympathy may not be the best way to get attention, but it is one way. Those who have gotten it for a number of years begin to realize that without it they would have no real means of forcing people to pay attention to them.

The man at Bethesda was such a man. I forced him to decide. It was as though I said to him, "I can give you legs and bid you walk away from this fruitless angel-watching. But of course, once you start getting about on your own, you will be expected to get a job and enter the dog-eat-dog world. There everyone has enough worries of their own to keep them from continually asking how your spleen is doing or if your arthritis is better. Being whole can set you free, but it will also leave you responsible. Is this what you really want? Do you want to be well?"

The man at the pool, after thinking it over, said yes.

I made him whole.

I will not tell you what became of the man. He walked away from the pool and the Scripture story closes there. But the world has never run out of those who are constantly in the process of deciding just how well they want to be.

I want to encourage you to begin to ask yourself this: What is the highest mark of your spiritual maturity? You are most mature when you minister to others in their pain without reminding them that you yourself have problems. Try to exalt others rather than trying to get them to exalt you.

Remember my cross and renounce all self-pity. As much as you can, ignore your own hurt and care for the needs of others. To minister to others when you yourself need ministry is to be liberated from all addictions to yourself.

LORD JESUS,
I want to triumph over
my need to control others.
I want to give attention rather than require it.
Help me to remember that in your pain,
you turned outward to the needs of those around your cross.
Then in my own pain, help me serve

and care for others while I stand,
recalling how you cared while hanging by your hands.
Amen.

52

TAKING THE REST
OUT OF THE DAY OF REST

LUKE 6:1-2
Now it came about that on a certain Sabbath He was passing through some grainfields; and His disciples were picking and eating the heads of grain, rubbing them in their hands. But some of the Pharisees said, "Why do you do what is not lawful on the Sabbath?"

LORD,
life is such a hassle. I'm tired most of the time. I get up tired. I go to bed tired. Is life supposed to be an endless season of fatigue?

Sabbath is the answer to your need. God made the Sabbath to take the tiredness out of your tired way of life.

The word *shavath* or *Sabbath* is the Hebrew word for the number seven. But it has through the ages also come to mean *rest*. If you have any need in this stressed-out century, you must rediscover the word *Sabbath*. Sabbath results in true rest. Most people in your generation are addicted to the pursuit of leisure, but few are really addicted to rest. But do not mistake these two words. Leisure is time off work. Rest is the restoration of the soul—the rebuilding of all that is torn and broken.

I did not say, "Come to me, and I will give you leisure!" In fact, if you come to me, I will not give you more time off. What I promise you is rest. Rest is that deep quality of "rightness" in life. It is not freedom from getting tired but the presence of joy that removes the ache of your meaningless fatigue. Real rest—true Sabbath—can even enjoy fatigue, for it knows you became tired while serving God's worthwhile aims.

It is not merely your toil that most longs for rest. It is the empty, meaningless toil that cries hardest for my rest. When you struggle with the great burdens of ministry, enjoy their labor. Avoid pointless labor, for pointless labor is busywork, empty of reason and filled with fatigue.

In classic mythology there is a story of a man named Sisyphus. All through his eternal existence in Hades, he was sentenced to roll a huge boulder up a mountain, and when he had it at the top, he had to release it and watch it roll down again. Then once more he would go to the bottom and push it up again. This was hell for Sysiphus—not because the work was hard but because it was pointless.

Salvation is rest, not because it calls believers to leisure but because, for the first time in their pointless lives, souls are able to work hard, believing that what they are doing really matters. They are serving me, and such service is the currency of eternity.

Are you tired? Do you need rest?

Realize that God, as a matter of principle, has established the Sabbath. It is only one day in seven, but it is so much more than that. It is the coming to a quiet place in your life each week and meeting with me for a deep drink of my Spirit. In my presence all your wounds made ragged by the grind will at last find healing. Let your own Sabbath celebrations bring you laughter and let that holy laughter repair your weary soul.

LORD JESUS,
help me remember that you, the Lord of the Sabbath, said,
"Come unto me, and I will give you rest."
Help me never to be guilty of taking the wonderful,
weekly respite of your day
and making it as hassled as all the rest.

And help me see that on such restful days,
I must lay by my toil, be washed by praise.
Amen.

53

HEALING MEN
OR RESCUING SHEEP

MATTHEW 12:9-14

And departing from there, He went into their synagogue. And behold, there was a man with a withered hand. And they questioned Him, saying, "Is it lawful to heal on the Sabbath?"—in order that they might accuse Him. And He said to them, "What man shall there be among you, who shall have one sheep, and if it falls into a pit on the Sabbath, will he not take hold of it, and lift it out? Of how much more value then is a man than a sheep! So then, it is lawful to do good on the Sabbath."

Then He said to the man, "Stretch out your hand!" And he stretched it out, and it was restored to normal, like the other. But the Pharisees went out, and counseled together against Him, as to how they might destroy Him.

LORD, the church seems to have so many rules, and the church seems to say that only if I keep them all will I ever be truly happy. Which rules, Lord, should I keep? Which ones will make me truly happy?

Happiness is rarely found in law. Even when the law is right, the pleasure of keeping it may seem joyless. But much of the time rules don't add up to happiness. Sometimes they just add up to legalisms. Legalisms are human extensions of the laws of God. Beware of them.

Legalisms are so reflexive, so dull and habitual, they rarely stop and listen to the imagination of heaven. The Pharisees publicly agreed that men were more valuable to God than sheep. But they had their set of rules, one of which said, don't heal on the Sabbath—*period*. There were no Pharisaical tables comparing the relative values of sheep and people. But there were many laws, hundreds of them expanding the fourth commandment. If you were going to keep the Sabbath holy, there were certain things you could not do. Healing on the Sabbath was one of them.

Good people can get confused about the meaning of life. In many churches, old taboos forbade Christians to be frivolous or play parlor games. These taboos were nowhere established by Scripture, yet they denounced various activities as incompatible with devotion. Whether right or wrong, they got fixed firmly as rules for the godly to obey. Such churches believed that good Christians always honored these fervent legalisms. Had God ever asked this of them? No, but the rules seemed to have come from people who said they knew God very well. They always assured their peers that God felt as they did about parlor games and frivolity.

So it was in my day that the Pharisees said, "Good Jews don't heal on the Sabbath." Who said so, the Torah? No, only very devoted scholars who had studied the Torah. The Pharisees were really saying, "When you get to know God as well as we do, you will be of our opinion."

Remember that legalisms are the words of man added to the Word of God. If God has banned any activity or indulgence and labeled it as sin, then surely it must be so. But what of those sins that some very good friends of God call sin?

So the Pharisees in my day went home thanking God that they, unlike the field rabbi of Nazareth, had never healed on the Sabbath. They believed this little law of their own making consecrated them to God. But God was rejoicing that night because a poor man he loved had suddenly found the perfectly good use of his hand. The joy in heaven that night was much greater than the sour righteousness of those grumbling legalists.

Give yourself only to the greatness of God. Live only for honest joy. Pledge yourself to find the heart of God. Be joyful even in the face of human pettiness. Joy meets God in the moment but holds him forever.

LORD JESUS,
help me remember I cannot expect
to see you do many great things
if I am always rehearsing little rules,
which I am told will please you.
God, I don't want to die having kept your vast freedom
in my little pockets.

I pledge myself to all that's great today,
with nothing small or stingy in the way.
Amen.

54

THE GENTLE, COMMITTED REDEEMER

MATTHEW 12:15-21

But Jesus, aware of this, withdrew from there. And many followed Him, and He healed them all, and warned them not to make Him known, in order that what was spoken through Isaiah the prophet, might be fulfilled, saying,

> Behold, My Servant, whom I have chosen;
> My Beloved in whom My soul is well-pleased;
> I will put My Spirit upon Him,
> And He shall proclaim justice to the Gentiles.
> He will not quarrel, nor cry out;
> Nor will anyone hear His voice in the streets.
> A battered reed He will not break off,
> And a smoldering wick He will not put out,
> Until He leads justice to victory.
> And in His name the Gentiles will hope.

LORD, the world is a brutal place. There's a harshness in humanity that makes us fear the marketplace. People seem hard of face and almost cruel at times. How can I beat the rap? How can I become what I seldom see in others? You are the author of the gentle, noble, human spirit. Teach me how it is to be done.

Be a gentle soul who loves with fervor. This passage from Isaiah will tell you of my coming, and you need to honor these two clear objectives. First, I came to present the gentleness of God in utter humility. This agenda was important to my Father. It now belongs to you. The world has had its share of warlords who have murdered their way to the chief seats of political kingdoms. But for once in history I would show the world that humility and kindness were the chief agendas of God. No roughshod military maneuvers or murderous tactics would establish God's gentle King in his gentle kingdom. But my way of life is now your way of life.

The second agenda was that I should not be deflected from my plan of world redemption. Those I healed knew I was from God; they were once sick and now were gloriously well. But they could not sense the size of my cosmic role in their small worldview. So I often forbade them to publish their opinions of how they viewed me, for they saw me too often as merely a here-and-now miracle worker. Their utter openness might prematurely force me to face the cross. The whole event of human redemption was on a time course that they could not understand. Not understanding it, they could not be allowed to alter the timeline or delay the grand cosmic design of human redemption.

The words of Isaiah really state your own purpose in living out my incarnation. Filled with the Spirit, you are now called to bring innocent kindness to your world. My cross came squarely in the middle of time. I was determined it would not fail. But I also knew I would conquer the harsh planet with an up-front gentleness. I would not allow myself to bruise a reed or snuff a lamp wick. I would be faithful.

Thus my course was set.

So is yours.

Gentleness is exhausting work.

Always keep your praise close at hand.

LORD JESUS,
how shall I thank you for loving me
enough to buy my soul at Calvary?
The expense was so great,
and I relish knowing what you paid for me.
Not that I am worth it
but that you esteemed me so.

I am redeemed as precious growing seed,
by gentleness that would not break a reed.
Amen.

55

CLAY LEADERSHIP

MARK 3:16

And He appointed the twelve: Simon (to whom He gave the name Peter)...

LORD,
I am so fickle in the promises I make to you. I find my resolve is froth. I can't seem to be consistent in my desire to put you first.

I suspect you are not much different from all those who have followed me. Consider the apostles. Of all those I appointed, Simon Peter was much like you describe yourself. He was clay, unsure of himself, sometimes bumbling and sometimes stalwart in what he tried to accomplish.

Peter could be loud and arrogant, but he was, in his best moments, a lover of God. He was so impulsive on the Mount of Transfiguration that he wanted to build three tents and stay there forever. His devotion was reckless but wonderfully warm. I once had to rebuke him for claiming to be able to accomplish more than he could actually perform. But Peter was the first disciple to confess me as the Christ.

His professions were as real as his weaknesses. He once tried to walk to me on the sea and failed. He once claimed he would never deny me and failed at that too. But he was not the sort to hide his faults. He always sinned right out in the open.

That is one of the reasons why I chose Peter as the leader of my church.

He had a habit of looking at me with this incredulous, childlike faith. He confessed me in love so often that it was easy to see that his devotion would triumph when his logic could not find a way. And if you could have seen him preaching on the Day of Pentecost, you would know why he was so essential to the Christian faith. He was only a fisherman, but he was destined to outperform the most polished rhetoricians. When he told the truth, hell trembled.

Your impulsiveness too is usable. After all, you desire to serve me without any duplicity. I believe you will live up to all you claim. Just go on giving me your ineptitude. I can easily make of you a bulwark of faith.

I would rather have your self-contempt for your lack of steadfastness than your overconfident surety that you will never fail me. You see, your distrust of your weakness keeps you dependent on me. As long as you see you can't handle life, I will be your source of strength. And when I have made you strong, you will live at a level of steadfastness you never dreamed possible.

LORD JESUS,
I surrender all within me that is reckless
and impulsive.
Forgive me when I promise too much, too fast.
I need that life that is anchored
so I will not drift with my large professions
that sometimes result in little deeds.

Here is the hurried soul you once set free.
Anchor me in chains to Calvary.
Amen.

56

THE DUFFER'S ROLE MODELS

MARK 3:16-19
And He appointed the twelve: Simon (to whom He gave the name
Peter), and James, the son of Zebedee, and John the brother of
James (to them He gave the name Boanerges, which means, "Sons
of Thunder"); and Andrew, and Philip, and Bartholomew, and
Matthew, and Thomas, and James the son of Alphaeus, and
Thaddaeus, and Simon the Zealot; and Judas Iscariot, who also
betrayed Him.

LORD,
I will keep my company with those who cherish yours.
The company of the committed is the bridgehead of
life's best assault on the future.

Your company is mine. I treasure those souls I called to be the first
legions of the disciplined. Consider my entire list of apostles. On their backs
rested the Christian enterprise. The Gospel writers have presented them
fairly. Each of them are laid out for your scrutiny. At first glance they seem
to be an army of rogues. Thomas, of course, doubted I had risen from the
dead. James and John were so prejudiced against Samaritans, they wanted
to call down fire from heaven on their heads. Their fiery grudges were only
exceeded by their ambition: These "Sons of Thunder" also sent their mother
to ask me if they could be my two right-hand nobles—the dukes of
heaven—when I came into my kingdom. Matthew was a tax-gatherer, never
much respected by the run-of-the-mill Jews in his day. Simon the Zealot
and Matthew didn't get along too well since the Zealots were committed to
destroying the very government that employed tax-gatherers like Matthew.
Then there was Judas, the treasurer of our group, whose wandering loyalty
degenerated into treachery.

You might look at these men and ask, "Were these the best applicants
you could find to become world changers?" They were indeed. The Gospels
let you see them with all their spots and wrinkles. This should keep you
from placing them on pedestals so high that their character appears to be

somehow unreachable. The truth is they were a lot like you. You have their same propensities to success and failure. So if the kingdom is born in you, and if you mark the world for great change, you will find that you must do it with all the same insecurities and self-doubts they had. The kingdom of God has literally reached its arms round the world. Those who have brought this world to my redemption were not usually the richest, wisest, greatest, or brightest. But they were always people in love with me.

And after all, love is the fuel that drives the kingdom. I never set out to choose omnicompetent disciples. Instead I chose lovers. How much did they love me? Well, nearly all of them died as martyrs. And martyrs beget martyrs. Those they inspired died by hundreds and sometimes by thousands. Further, most of these—most of my first 12 disciples—died hundreds of miles from their Aramaic homelands. Only love will call people to go such distances and die such deaths.

So they were more extraordinary than you may have imagined. My love forged their weakness into steel. My love can also put some steel in your resolve. The rogues they appeared to be stood at last in the flames, sometimes singing their way into eternity. So walk with me. In my company, you will end up a role model of steadfast triumph.

LORD JESUS,
I am amazed what ordinary people can do.
I used to believe that there was no real place
for me in this extraordinary kingdom.
Now I know the truth:
Saints were never heroes in their own eyes.

I offer you my own unworthy clay.
Make of me unyielding steel today.
Amen.

ON LOVING TRAITORS

MARK 3:19
...and Judas Iscariot, who also betrayed Him.

LORD,
how much am I like Judas?

Not much! But in one way you are alike. You were both the beloved of God.

Judas' spot at the end of the apostles' list does not imply that he ever suffered from a lack of love. He did not. He did betray me and end his life with suicide, but his final plight did not escape the reaching heart of heaven. Judas was not lost because God hated him but because his self-concern always kept him living too much in the center of his own arrogance.

Judas loved Judas. He was so bound up in what he wanted for Judas, he could not focus on what he wanted for me. It wasn't the 30 pieces of silver that he most wanted. He tried to give that back (Matthew 27:1-5). What he couldn't give back was his broken loyalty.

Judas broke everything and yet never became broken himself.

He broke trust.

He broke faith.

He broke covenants.

He broke every definition of loyalty.

What Judas did on Maundy Thursday was not much worse than what Peter did on the very same evening. They both denied me. And they both felt bad about what they had done. Peter's weeping at cockcrow was evidence that he felt bad. Judas's suicide was evidence that he also felt bad. But Peter wept in godly sorrow, eager to return to me for healing. Judas' disconsolation never found its object in repentance and confession. He died as he had lived—with too many agendas of his own.

Judas' name has become a synonym for treachery, Christianity's arch monster.

He died outside of grace for exactly the same reason that others do: He never committed his life to my lordship. Self was his great sin. He lived and died shut up in the narrow walls of his ego. Suicides often write their final notes on the small enclosures of their windowless souls.

Come away from Judas and live large. See the world outside your small affairs. That is the world I have died to save and you must live to serve.

LORD JESUS,
you are there when I need you.
Am I there when you need me?
You have never once betrayed me
in the middle of any desperate circumstances.
Help me to never betray you.

Lord, strengthen me with all that faith's about,
lest I, in treachery, should sell you out.
Amen.

58

BLESSED ARE THE POOR IN SPIRIT

MATTHEW 5:3
Blessed are the poor in spirit, for theirs is the kingdom of heaven.

LORD, the rich are self-sufficient. The poor have needs, and so I should not cherish poverty but bring my empty poverty of spirit to you and beg you to fill it.

Your poverty is not precious; you need to let me supply your poverty with spiritual riches. So hunger to be poor in spirit! This is an impoverishment to be celebrated! When your resources are short, you will bring your starving soul to me. So you must learn to cherish that poverty of spirit that blesses you and all who own its joyous state.

Let your poverty make for you a place in a needy brotherhood. Those who are poor know it. Their lives mark their need. But the poor have one treasure the rich rarely own: They know they need each other. Most of the poor find their needs met by other poor people. The wealthy rarely help the poor. It's because they really never see them. The wealthy are too much involved in their own affairs to look ahead. The wealthy rarely need anyone. Do not desire wealth, for wealth too often breeds an arrogance and a self-sufficiency that needs neither God nor anyone else.

You must turn from such self-sufficiency. The poor are more likely to share their last loaf than the rich are likely to give away anything from their full pantries. The wealthy lament the hard times as stopovers of ugly necessity, wedged between the good times where they manage to figure out their finances on their own. But the poor, knowing fewer good times, are much better at giving from their penury than the wealthy give from their abundance.

I once said, "It is hard for a rich man to enter the kingdom of heaven. Again I tell you, it is easier for a camel to go through the eye of a needle than for a rich man to enter the kingdom of God" (Matthew 19:23-24).

After meeting a rich man who wanted to be my disciple but simply felt he had too much wealth to give away, I said, "If you want to be perfect, go, sell your possessions, and give to the poor, and you will have treasure in heaven" (Matthew 19:21). Alas, the rich rarely value heavenly treasure. They remain addicted to simpler and poorer forms of wealth.

But you are to treasure heaven because to the poor in spirit, heaven is everything. The poor talk of it and sing of it in their assemblies. They joyously rehearse their future wealth in eternity.

Who then is really rich? You are if you do not turn from being poor in spirit! You will be rich both in this world and the one to come. But you will be the "needy rich," and you will understand that it is your need that has made you rich.

LORD JESUS,
make me destitute of spirit
so I may treasure that true wealth
that comes from you only.
I want to be so needy that I find
all my sufficiency in you alone.

My heart is empty-pocketed. So fold
me into riches where there's wealth untold.
Amen.

59

BLESSED ARE THE GENTLE

MATTHEW 5:5
Blessed are the gentle, for they shall inherit the earth.

LORD,
if gentleness will let anyone approach me, I will be gentle. I want to be like a child (who is too small and soft to hurt anyone) so all may approach and touch me without fear.

You have desired a good thing. The gentle have long suffered at the hands of the fierce and the cruel. If heaven knows any automatic mood, it feels an instant love for all the gentle souls whose quiet natures so often become the targets of the power-mad and depraved. Humanity's inhumanity is the stuff that makes God cry. Gentle souls are like children. Indeed, they are the children of God.

But you must not see the gentility of the gentle as the result of their victimization by the powerful. No, they were not made gentle by being stripped of power. In the best cases, gentility was not forced upon them; it was an option that they chose. They treasured that open state of living so that no one ever need be afraid of them.

Let a child guide you to be gentle. No one fools a child. Innocence can guess at once what guilt can never locate: true, approachable kindness. So when a child snuggles in against the breast of a complete stranger, he has flawlessly pointed you to the life of gentility.

But if you want a picture of gentility that conquers power, you must go to my cross. There you will see what power can do to the gentle and how gentleness responds. For in that moment when I was naked and bereft before Pilate, I did not accuse in return. I was, as Isaiah said, a lamb silent before its shearers.

I was gentle. Yet I had the power to knock the planet to pieces. I could have called ten thousand angels to destroy the world, but I did not. Gentility is never weakness. It is power under control. Few really gentle people are weak. They have simply learned to subdue their baser nature. They know how bad it feels to feel bad. They have determined that they would rather receive abuse than offer it. They are people of such extraordinary power, they thrill at the disciplines they mastered to become gentle.

Pattern your life in all your relationships like the rider of a huge stallion. You may ride it like a warlord, trampling all of those who get in your way. Or you may choose to be gentle. Those who choose to be gentle have reined the stallion of ego into submission. Their lust for dominance is under complete control. They have shackled the steed of their heavy-handedness, and their world is blessed.

Blessed are the gentle.

Blessed. Blessed. Blessed.

LORD JESUS,
help me to live so gently
that none are afraid of me.
Help me to lay all needs for power
at your feet.
And when I have placed them there,
I will notice that your feet were wounded.
Then with this offering I will remember,
gentility is always at the mercy of despots.

So may your blood remind me of my need
to suffer wounds that others may not bleed.
Amen.

60

BLESSED IS A GOOD APPETITE

MATTHEW 5:6-7
Blessed are those who hunger and thirst for righteousness, for they
shall be satisfied. Blessed are the merciful, for they shall receive
mercy.

LORD,
it's a little thing, but the grocer gave me change for a $50
when he should have only given me change for a $20. It
would have been an easy way for me to make 30 bucks.
Oh, I told him about it. Mostly because I couldn't bear
the thought of him making up his mistake out of his
own salary...or maybe worse, getting fired. Doing the
right thing is not as easy as I would like it to be.

Integrity is the virtue of heaven. It is the summation of the last five
commandments. No human appetite is so glorious to God as the hunger
for righteousness. The world is morally bankrupt, and the gold that redeems
it from its bankruptcy is righteousness. And what is righteousness?
Righteousness is holiness in longing. And holiness is a hunger for God's
approval. It is a craving for wholeness. It is a reaching out after the moral
God. Blessed are you who care about holiness, for it is the character of God.

But righteousness is elusive. People are the sum total of their appetites.
They talk most about what they most hunger for. If they hunger for material things, they will talk of shopping sprees or ramble on and on about the
things they own. If they are gluttons, they will talk, even as they eat, of what
they have eaten at other times and places. If they are addicted to sexual
desires, they will spin endless stories of their caprice and brag of those times
they indulged their hearts in the illicit.

Hunger makes you serve yourselves to devour all you are hungry for.
Hunger drives you till you fill your need.
Hunger makes you yearn for what you cannot live without.
Many people's appetites drive them to addictions, detox wards, or 12-
step programs. But some appetites end in glory. These appetites belong to

those whose affections are hidden in their love for me. Such appetites are inward; still, they speak incessantly of me. Many who study my teachings call themselves Christian. But few hunger and thirst after righteousness. In such hearts the longing to please me is insatiable.

Hungering after righteousness is a glorious and restless appetite. Are you marked by such a hunger? Bless that hunger. Such an acknowledgment reveals your appetite for God. Such compulsions put the gold in the streets of heaven.

LORD JESUS,
you were tempted in all ways, yet you lived without sin.
This was not your burden but your desire of joy.
Forgive me for sometimes considering righteousness
as though it were a headache.
Forgive me for considering it to be an awful
but necessary burden.
Help me crave integrity so that I can claim
my kinship with the character of God.

Confirm my needy hunger for the light,
and whet my better, honest appetites.
Amen.

61

BLESSED ARE THE INNOCENT, NOT THE NAIVE

MATTHEW 5:8
Blessed are the pure in heart, for they shall see God.

LORD,
it is such a swanky and sophisticated age...and here I am in the midst of it. People like me appear naive and void of the one-size-fits-all morality. So many seem to flirt with edgy lifestyles; they are applauded for their compromises and proud of their side deals with ambition. I would like to appear more with-it. I hate being seen as naive. Can anything be done to give me a more worldly-wise reputation?

Being accused of naïveté is not a compliment. The naive are not pure in heart; they are just people who don't understand the complexity of life. The naive are those who have no real experience and therefore have made their judgments on how to live on the basis of other people's experience. They have not decided to be pure in heart; they just blunder into what appears a strong moral life but isn't.

Naïveté to some degree is willful ignorance.

Innocence is a matter of choice. It recognizes evil but chooses not to serve it. Innocence is Adam in Eden, newly created to enjoy God forever. Still wet and dripping as divine clay, innocence was fresh-formed from the mold of God and shaped in the heat of love. Adam knew there was such a thing as sin, but he had not yet imagined its consequence in his heart. He was a child, a man, both. He loved his Maker with that purity of conscience that never stopped to play with any notion of betrayal. He was as innocent, holy, and pure as the Creator he adored.

And in this innocence Adam daily met his holy Maker. He had nothing to hide yet, no apple cores of guilt. He was in love with God, feasting daily on the bread of his choice not to taste the forbidden. Adam slept as sleep should be defined. Nothing nagged his peace.

Innocence is rest. Innocence is cleanness. Innocence is a clear, unfogged mirror into which the true believer stares and finds God staring back. Innocence may be had in two ways. You are born with it. Indeed, you consciously choose to give it up when you sin. Iniquity, on the other hand, is the practice of honoring your edgy preferences. Finally Adam reached for the apple of power and scrapped his innocence in favor of ambition.

Do you hunger to be pure in heart? If so, the only kind of innocence left is that which I confer upon you by my own sinlessness. In my sinless sacrifice, a new kind of righteousness became possible. It is imputed righteousness (Romans 5). What did the apostle Paul mean by imputed righteousness? He meant that there is a kind of righteousness beyond the kind you may be trying to manufacture on your own. It is hard work to try to live up to the expectation of the Ten Commandments. Indeed, it is impossible. Since it cannot be done, all your attempts at perfection can only leave you with feelings of guilt and failure. Since you cannot perfectly keep the law, you must seek out a kind of righteousness from God that comes from my sinlessness. It is a kind of sinlessness you could never achieve on your own.

To walk in holiness is to take that holy innocence that I achieved by sinless living and place it in the center of your own soiled life. This imputed righteousness is available to you merely for the desiring. Do you desire it? Will you ask for it that you may receive it? Will you seek it that you may find it? Will you knock that such a door may be opened to you?

LORD JESUS,
I come to you with my fruit half eaten.
I hide the seeds of my disobedience.
And even while I promise you
I will eat such sickly fruit no more,
I am planting yesterday's seeds so I can replenish my guilt
with tomorrow's sins.
Forgive my hypocrisy.
Cleanse me.

So come. Take from my life its ugly parts
and furnish me with purity of heart.
Amen.

62

THE DANGEROUS WORK OF PEACE-MAKING

MATTHEW 5:9 (KJV)
Blessed are the peacemakers: for they shall be called the children of God.

LORD,
making peace means I must step outside the warmth I feel from living with my own comfortable viewpoints. I like my friends. My friends have my kind of values, hold my philosophies, and recite my creeds. To become a peacemaker I must come between warring factions and bid them seek some middle way. It's painful work to separate dogs whose snarling can fall on me if I try to teach them compromise.

Separating quarreling dogs is dangerous. Wherever hate rages, peace-makers face injury. Peacemaking is what my cross was all about. At Calvary, God and humankind were at odds. Of course, few ever said they hated God, but God and humanity were separated because of the way they felt about me. So I came as a peacemaker, a reconciler. I drove my cross between humanity's horrid apathy and God's raging love. My hands and feet are still marked by the price I paid.

So my advice to you is this: Take up your cross and continue my work of reconciling. You too must have the courage at times to step between the apathetic world and longing grace.

Most people spend their lives dividing their world into friends and enemies. They seem to believe that if only they could eliminate all the people they don't like, all of those left would be their friends. Peacemakers never serve such myths. They know the only way to rid the world of their enemies is to rename their foes as friends.

Your antagonists can never be killed in sufficient numbers to rid your world of all your enemies. Your key to interpersonal peace lies in how you draw your circles. When people draw you out of some hard, exclusive circle, redraw a bigger, more inclusive circle and take them in. A reconciler is one who enjoys the art of large circles.

Two soldiers, enemies in humanity's everlasting war, fell on the same part of a wide battlefield. These wounded, dying foes fell into the same foxhole. As they died, the strong lure of family marked their final moments. Each of them drew from their clothes pictures of their families in order to take a last, lingering look. Then, though they didn't know each other's languages, each showed the other his pictures. Even though they wore the uniforms of foes, this epiphany of insight taught them they were not different enough to be enemies. In their final moments of life they drew circles of inclusion. Thus, they died friends.

Circle drawing is the peacemaker's ploy. Grudges and war can only exist in smaller provinces of spite. So enlarge your grace. Make your circles ever greater. Bigger circles will in time save the world.

LORD JESUS,
I have too much loved the camps in which I serve.
I like my small collection of friends too much
to advise them.
I would rather join them in their animosities
than challenge them to live more tolerant of our common enemies.
Help me to say the word peacemaker *every morning,*
with the understanding of the cost of alienation
I must pay right now.

Help me to tell my friends, "Let hatred cease…
Draw larger circles of enduring peace."
Amen.

63

PURPOSEFUL SCARS

MATTHEW 5:10 (KJV)
Blessed are they which are persecuted for righteousness' sake: for
theirs is the kingdom of heaven.

LORD,
I love the scars of those who found their wounds pursuing some great dream. Every noble scar is a mark of
heroism. But those who bear such scars were rarely
heroes to themselves. They only did what honesty
required. Thus came their wounds. Then their scars.
Then their sheer nobility. Am I living too much in fear
of wounds to produce any noble scars?

Your moment for the stand will come. Your scars are on the way. Neither
avoid the moment that you win the badge, nor seek to hasten it.

The word *martyr* might be defined as "the very best friend God has."
Crave the word as you would crave the scars. The literal meaning of the
word *martyr* is "witness." Martyrs know no shallow definition of love.
Martyrs make public their allegiance to my name. A martyr will say "Jesus
is Lord" anytime, anywhere, regardless of the consequences. You may stand
her at a stake if you wish. But even as you pile the matchwood about her
feet, she will not change her mind, for she has chosen to wear the noble
name of *martyr*. She will sing her own requiem, embarrassed that she has
nothing greater to give God than her life.

Be a witness. You must never feel uncomfortable among those who love
me to the point of the winning scars. Always speak openly of your love for
me. Never hide our relationship. Let your witness be the seal of our love.
Other kinds of commitment have their own symbols; let your devotion
become the symbol of your love for me. Those who are married wear a
wedding ring. Soldiers unashamedly wear uniforms. Martyrs confess, and
their confession is the signet of their allegiance. You are mine. Show it!

That which is real cannot be hidden. Great truths have an energy about
them that releases them from their confinement in small minds. If you can

hide your faith to escape persecution, it is only because your faith is small enough to be concealed.

Take a lesson from children. They love their parents so much they cannot hide their love. You are my child. Are you afraid of persecution? Does social ostracism frighten you? If so, remember this: Your exclusion or acceptance by other human beings is of no real eternal consequence. If you are persecuted for me, you are blessed. I was once persecuted for you. Let your persecutions—great or small—become our fellowship of suffering (Philippians 4:14), for the servant is not greater than his Lord, neither is he that is sent greater than he that sent him (John 15:20).

LORD JESUS,
the next time I tell someone I am a witness,
Help me to remember that martyr
is the New Testament word for all I claim to be.
Upon the force of this better definition,

help me to kneel and bless your holy name,
to always be what I so quickly claim.
Amen.

64

THE FALSELY ACCUSED

MATTHEW 5:11-12

Blessed are you when men cast insults at you, and persecute you, and say all kinds of evil against you falsely, on account of Me. Rejoice, and be glad, for your reward in heaven is great, for so they persecuted the prophets who were before you.

LORD, today I learned that a colleague—whom I much admired—has gossiped about me, spreading lies that I cannot tolerate. I want to burn his house down and tell him what I think of his lies. Is this wrong? What am I to do?

Do nothing in anger. Manage your rage. Renovate your heart. Your antagonist is only your enemy as long as you allow him to be. The ill-will you bear him is not of his making. It grows inside you with your permission. You can't hope to win by giving him a volley of returned hurt. You win by buying him coffee and asking about his family.

Remember, before the mob on Good Friday, I felt the pain of false accusation. If ever there was a travesty of justice, this must have been it. Little of all that was brought against me was true. Above my cross was a sign written in three languages: "Jesus of Nazareth, the king of the Jews." This *titulus* of accusation was truer than my enemies understood. For they meant it only as a mockery and slur.

But examine my deportment. I did not rail against the railers. I did not try to outshout those who raged against me. Protesting our innocence, even when it is just, is rarely effective. In the midst of these blasphemous allegations I turned to my heavenly Father. I could hear my Father saying over and over, "The treachery of your accusers is false. You are my only begotten Son, in whom I am well pleased."

Justifying yourselves before your accusers will do little good. They will only accuse you all the more. Instead, take your innocence into the prayer closet. Meet me there, and you will enjoy my affirmation even during the

131

accusations of your enemies. The affirmation of God is sweet in the midst of human treachery. It is the only balm that heals the deepest hurt.

A blessing is hidden in the pain of your ostracism. It is this: Only when you are utterly rejected will you turn to me for friendship. As long as you have one earthly friend who will sympathize with your miserable estate, you will not celebrate my friendship. If you have any other human counsel, you will fail to seek my own.

Can you see why martyrs sang at flaming stakes? In the midst of human contempt they knew that ostracism is really the final friend of faith.

If you could, you would choose a life free of ostracism and criticism. But I would rather you know rejection and need me, than to live a life of such wide acceptance you never needed me. In the wounds of ostracism lies your own maturity. What maturity? Our unbreakable union as wounded lovers. When I, the wounded King, meet you, my wounded subject, you and I enter into holy union. Seek that union. It satisfies me. Let it satisfy you.

LORD JESUS,
thank you for being quietly
in the middle of raucous accusation.
Help me to take my petty wounds into the closet
of prayer.
I want to meet you there and linger until I am past all forgetting
that there is only one tribunal.
It has never been on earth.
It has never been wrong.

I enter into silence, knowing there,
your Spirit always stirs the waiting air.
Amen.

65

THE SALT AND LIGHT PEOPLE

MATTHEW 5:13-16

You are the salt of the earth; but if the salt has become tasteless, how will it be made salty again? It is good for nothing anymore, except to be thrown out and trampled under foot by men.

You are the light of the world. A city set on a hill cannot be hidden. Nor do men light a lamp, and put it under the peck-measure, but on the lampstand; and it gives light to all who are in the house.

Let your light shine before men in such a way that they may see your good works, and glorify your Father who is in heaven.

LORD, I've hit the wall. Who am I? Why am I here? There must be a reason. Why am I forced to live on a planet whose people I can't understand? What am I doing here besides eating and breathing?

You are salt, you are light. You are here to flavor and illuminate this dark world you call home.

When my Father created light, he commanded it to be exhibitionist. When the sun shucks off the mists of night, her darksome garments fall shamelessly away. Light cannot hide. It is by very nature a show-off. Light tells all. It is the bright braggart—wild and uncontainable—knowing no secrets.

Genesis 1 says it all: *"Fiat lux!"* "Let there be light!" With such a mandate given to light, the darkness had no choice but to sneak off to the dingier corners of the universe. "Let there be light"…simple words, yet those words spoke into being a substance that physicists have never explained. Light is the glorious stuff of all cosmic energy. It lets us see the growing edges of the universe. It gathers its spectral soul into rainbows and sticks its peacock brilliance into Magellanic Clouds a thousand light-years wide.

But best of all, light warms, illuminates, discloses, and reveals. It can focus in laser beams of glory to cut the blindness from the blind. It can show a miner his way into the heart of the earth. It lives in lighthouses to warn mariners of reefs. It displays the wonders of the deep and rushes rockets to the edges of the cosmos.

But perhaps the best thing about light is that it rarely serves itself. It fills your world to make vision possible, yet it is so transparent you never see it. It is like the air that fills your lungs with life for scores of years yet is never seen. Light too is always there, serving you by making the world seeable yet itself invisible to the eye. And the only time you ever stop to think of light is when darkness closes in. Then at last you crave light. Then you beg for it.

You are light, I tell you! You are filled with my being, and you have become the brilliance that helps the world locate its soul and shine on culture's bogus values. Light convicts. When you enter a dark but messy room, you do not have to rebuke either the darkness or the mess. All you have to do is to turn on the light. The light will reprimand the mess.

So walk in the light, and perhaps your world will see well enough to give up its addiction to evil.

LORD JESUS,
there is a thin but elusive threshold
between those who are obnoxiously outward about faith
and those who are cowardly and ashamed to bear witness.
Help me not to blind people with my own inner light,
but help me never hide it either.

I must remind myself that sight
can't come to those intent on hiding light.
Amen.

66

Making Friends With the Bible

Matthew 5:17-18

Do not think that I am come to abolish the Law or the Prophets; I did not come to abolish, but to fulfill. For truly I say to you, until heaven and earth pass away, not the smallest letter or stroke shall pass away from the Law, until all is accomplished.

LORD,
I find the Bible nearly obtuse at times. I try to understand, but I can't. What did all these ancient people have to do with my jet-set life? I need it, but it seems a "thee and thou" intrusion into my entrepreneurial worldview. It's the Old Testament mostly. Is it all that necessary? I can't make it relate. Help me.

You must try to see the Bible as a whole. If you separate it into parts and allow yourself to name some parts of it interesting and some as boring, it will always seem irrelevant to you.

The God of the Old Testament never changed his mind as he wrote the New. Never! Heretics in every era have taught that the Hebrew Scriptures were a mistake that God had to correct later with updated ideas. Not so! The Ten Commandments were not just a set of rules God gave to make the world nervous. They are timeless definitions. Murder is forever wrong. Theft too. Lying, coveting, failing to love God and honor parents: These are sins in any day.

Grace came with me. But I never said that murder in the New Testament era was less serious than it had been in the Old Testament. What I was saying was that killing was not simply a matter of murder, but a deeper issue rooted in grudge and anger. Obeying the law is good, but that hungering after a spiritual nature—where murder is not possible—is even better. My teachings are an attempt to get others to live morally by focusing on right rather than wrong.

Make a note of this: The Bible isn't primarily about ancient peoples. It is about you. You are going to meet with many moral obstacles while trying to live a worthy life. But if you think that moral living is a matter of avoiding sin, you will be dogged by negative preoccupations. If, however, you focus on the joy of pleasing the Teacher, you will achieve a joyous way of life. The road map for your journey will be Scripture, all the Scripture. And no part of it will be unrelated.

In the same way, if you want to avoid cheating on your marriage vows, you should not walk around focusing on all the possible consorts you must be strong enough to refuse. You need only take home flowers once a week and affirm your lifelong mate with compliments and love. In doing this you will strengthen your own romance with a fervor that will preclude all betrayal.

There are plenty of insights to be gleaned from those ancient men and women who gave you the Bible. Never ignore their wisdom. The better you understand the Bible, the more you and I will come together in oneness and the more disobedience will lose its appeal to you. Our friendship will become the chief pursuit of your life, and the Scripture will affirm our friendship. Pursue the ancient wisdom! In doing this you will have walked away from sin, and the values you have found will be ancient, tried, and true.

LORD JESUS,
help me to follow all the commandments
and prove what acts are right,
but help me to follow you to find that life
in which sin is impossible
because I hunger too much for your presence.
Help me not try to arrive at righteousness
by trying to quit what is wrong,
but to arrive there by honoring the ancient words.

I cannot conquer sin or struggle through
what I might gain by simply loving you.
Amen.

67

THE DEMON'S FATHER

MATTHEW 5:21-24

You have heard that the ancients were told, "You shall not commit murder" and "Whoever commits murder shall be liable to the court." But I say to you that everyone who is angry with his brother shall be guilty before the court; and whoever shall say to his brother, "Raca," shall be guilty before the supreme court; and whoever shall say, "You fool," shall be guilty enough to go into the fiery hell. If therefore you are presenting your offering at the altar, and there remember that your brother has something against you, leave your offering there before the altar, and go your way; first be reconciled to your brother, and then come and present your offering.

LORD,
I can't help but lose my temper sometimes. But it's not so bad, is it? Anger is, after all, one of the four basic emotions. If being a Christian means never being angry, I'll never be a Christian. People drive me crazy. I just get angry, that's all.

Anger is basic, but stay in charge. If you never lose control, murder will always be a stranger to you. Murder is only a grudge that has lost all self-control.

Walk gently in your world. If someone offends you, take charge of the fury that tries to lash back. It is not just that your unbridled temper might hurt someone else. Uncontrolled anger will in time kill you as well. It kills you by first denying you a focus on all that is rational and productive. Anger destroys you by leaving your good reputation at the mercy of your tantrums.

Do not give my Father any gift while you are angry with another. It is the divided heart that claims to love God while it holds a grudge toward anyone. "If someone says, 'I love God,' and hates his brother, he is a liar; for the one who does not love his brother whom he has seen, cannot love God whom he has not seen" (1 John 4:20).

It is a sin to know me and not add to yourself the discipline of self-control. Yet grudges are common. Even denominations have been guilty of holding grudges toward those who seem to have gotten some of their doctrine wrong. Those who practice such grudges become little more than bookkeeping clubs, organized to protect someone's vested religious interests. These privatized Christian groups seem to feel as though I would be a part of their particular group if I were on earth today.

How false.

Do not separate the kingdom into small special communions. Bless anyone who loves me in any framework of ministry. Until you can freely give me your gifts in complete love for everyone, do not give me your gifts at all.

LORD JESUS,
it is the hardest lesson of my life
that I should not be selective and love too narrowly.
You have loved broadly,
so permit me to hold no malice at all.
Help me never to bring my offering of godly love
while I hold in my heart some ugly contempt.

Help me to lift all of your lovers up,
and bid them sip with me one glorious cup.
Amen.

68

THE HEART OF DARKNESS

MATTHEW 5:27-28
You have heard that it was said, "You shall not commit adultery";
but I say to you, that everyone who looks on a woman to lust for
her has committed adultery with her already in his heart.

LORD,
I don't like the word *lust*, probably because I protect the
fault within my heart and keep it much too close at
hand. My eye sins first and then bids my heart partici-
pate. And sometimes it grinds out images that war
against the world of my relationships. Lust sins the
inward sins and keeps itself well hidden. It is a human
fault. So should I feel so bad that I allow my heart to
harbor it? After all, the inner sins are common.

Lust is immoral. Lust is common. But never forget this: People are
sacred. All people! They are individual temples. Every human heart is the
dwelling place of God. The apostle reminds us, "Flee from sexual immorality. All other sins a man commits are outside his body, but he who sins sexu-
ally sins against his own body. Do you not know that your body is a temple
of the Holy Spirit, who is in you, whom you have received from God?"
(1 Corinthians 6:18-19 NIV).

Your heart is your highest, most sacred altar. Do not profane its holiness with inner indecency.

Lust is lurid, inner commerce. It undresses sacred people—other
temples of God—inside your own private holy place. There you violate
them with unseemly fantasies. It coaxes Ashtaroth into the company of the
Holy Spirit. It makes a common bed of sin and sanctity. The psalmist
reminds us that "a man's heart reflects the man" (Proverbs 27:19 NIV). Do
not suppose you may play the saint before the world but live a life of inner
license. Be wise. Your inner soul may in time betray the outer.

There is not room in one heart to contain both an attitude of godly
adoration and ungodly fantasies. When you give place to evil imaginings,

your own love for God must retreat into the smaller, darker corners of your heart. And if you live too much within this secret lust, you will find that your fantasies compel you to seek open betrayals. You then will disappoint your family. But these earthly disappointments will only be the capstone of what has disappointed your heavenly Father all along.

Your heart is more than a temple of lust; it is the theater of your future. The rehearsal of the drama that you have cherished in private will at last play before the open cinema of your disgrace. King David once watched Bathsheba at her bath. From this dark rehearsal of lust came his actual adultery. To hide his adultery he later murdered, stole, and lied.

Such is the fruit of the permissive imagining. Lust changes kings to gigolos. David hid from God. He traded righteousness for license. But every act of his outward immorality, he first rehearsed in the privacy of his heart.

What illicit dramas do you rehearse? What images do you play with in the inner cinema of your life? Come to purity. Make strong the temple at the center of your heart. Build an altar so large you've no room left to build a brothel there.

LORD JESUS,
Everyone is sacred.
Every body is a temple.
When my imaginings transgress the sanctity of any sacred being,
my own soul trades its gold for lead,
its iron truth for the rotted plaster of decaying sensuality.

Lord, make my fickle heart a worship space,
lest I give lust an easy bedding place.
Amen.

69

DIVIDING THE INDIVISIBLE

And it was said, "Whoever sends his wife away, let him give her a
certificate of divorce"; but I say to you that everyone who divorces
his wife, except for the cause of unchastity, makes her commit
adultery; and whoever marries a divorced woman commits
adultery.

LORD,
I have two married friends who are getting a divorce.
They just can't live together. They make each other
miserable. They're incompatible, as they say. They're
always at each other's throats. Wouldn't they be better
off to be free of each other and give themselves—and
the world around them—a little rest?

Are your friends selling marriage short? Do they recall the reasons God
founded marriage? Did they not once try to be one?

To divide anything that longs to be whole sins against unity. To cut the
roots of a great oak and separate them from the trunk in time destroys the
tree.

Marriage is the grafting of two souls into a wonderful, spiritual inter-
dependency. Life becomes a oneness that did not exist before a promise
made a single organism out of separateness. Marital love arrives where the
paths of mutual submission meet. When a man and a woman voluntarily
surrender their private agendas to each other, each promises enduring
commitment to the other's welfare. They vow that in sickness and health,
through ultimate trials of soul, they will live for each other.

But if they are not disciplined in their loving, divorce may divide them.
The lure of new passions will smother them in the ashes of their lost
integrity. Have they not promised, "for better, for worse, forever"? Then
why this voluntary selling of their souls to promote their own private agendas? Did they not agree that they would have no private agendas? Did they
not say, "What's mine is yours, and yours, mine"? Now, do they dare to take

back their words, reschedule their oaths, or sell their secondhand, shifty promises to some intriguing newcomer outside their former promises?

Mark this: There is no such thing as self-seeking love. The two terms cancel each other out. A marriage altar is a union of high promises, not the welding of errant self-interests. A man or woman who will promise and then break those promises has no chance of making better promises to someone else later. In fact, those who divorce and remarry are likely to divorce again. Why? Because they are fundamentally dishonest. They will not do what they say. They are mere hawkers of breathy candlelit promises, pandering high truths they have not the honesty to keep.

So when I said that he who divorces his wife sins, I was really saying this: All breakers of the holy union are committing sins of broken integrity. Think long and hard before you make a marriage promise. Then commit yourself to all you promise. If you say, "Till death do us part," never make secondary vows with lesser texts. Determine to be a person of integrity. Marriage is a magnificent submission.

LORD JESUS,
help me never to join that permissive
war of arrogance
by which the self-excusing
excuse themselves of their integrity.
Help me to honor every vow
and to mean it when I say,
"For better, for worse, forever."

I want to ward off marriage surgery,
by keeping all my vows from perjury.
Amen.

70

A LIE IS BUT
INFLATED TRUTH

MATTHEW 5:33-37

Again, you have heard that the ancients were told, "You shall not make false vows, but shall fulfill your vows to the Lord." But I say to you, make no oath at all, either by heaven, for it is the throne of God, or by the earth, for it is the footstool of His feet, or by Jerusalem, for it is the city of the great King. Nor shall you make an oath by your head, for you cannot make one hair white or black. But let your statement be, "Yes, yes" or "No, no"; and anything beyond these is of evil.

LORD, is it possible to speak so simply that I never need to swear to anyone that I am telling the truth? Shouldn't a person take some forceful stand for honesty? Can this not be done by enlarging my oath to speak in a swelling manner to convince my friends I tell the truth?

Your reputation must rest in simplicity.

It is a natural tendency to assure all those you meet that you are trustworthy. To do this, you may be tempted to preface or follow your statements with some verbal addendum that certifies your promises. How odd such overstatements sound. Some swear "on their mother's soul." Some swear "on a stack of Bibles" that they are telling the truth. Others "cross their heart and hope to die."

Beware the overstatement! Radical clichés never certify honesty. If anything, they call it into question. Character needs no certification. Yes and no are simple answers that bind consistency to trust.

Do not grow overly fond of the emphatic. Seek no hyperbole to certify your reply. Remember this: Simplicity bears its best message in character. When good people speak to you, they need no special oath. Their unchangeable character has already convinced you.

Abandon every tendency to make simple truth flamboyant. Lies always need heavy ornamentation to sell themselves as the truth. A heavily ornamental falsehood is rather like a woman who sells a house with holes in the walls. Rather than mending the walls, she covers each hole by hanging a picture over it. But to make extra sure that the suspecting buyer does not lift the pictures to look for holes, she hangs very big pictures over very small holes. Still she doubts, reasoning that even the big pictures might be moved to look for holes. Then she hangs only huge canvases in heavy plastered frames. Such heavy frames are not needed to keep the buyer from inspecting her integrity. But they are needed in her own mind to be sure she succeeds with her cover-ups.

Do not hang simple conversations in "oathy" frames. They make your integrity suspect. Good clean walls, on the other hand, will tell you the seller isn't hiding anything. So if you accidentally knock a hole in the wall, it is more honest to replaster with repentance than to hang up a lot of suspicious artwork.

LORD JESUS,
when you spoke the truth,
everyone knew it was the truth,
for you were the truth, the way, the life.
Help me to be so filled with you
that any hint of dishonesty
will be dispelled by your presence proclaiming itself from inside me.

I want my honesty in full display,
So let my nay be nay, my yea be yea.
Amen.

71

AN EYELESS,
TOOTHLESS WORLD

MATTHEW 5:38-42

You have heard that it was said, "An eye for an eye, and a tooth for a tooth." But I say to you, do not resist him who is evil; but whoever slaps you on your right cheek, turn to him the other also. And if anyone wants to sue you, and take your shirt, let him have your coat also. And whoever shall force you to go one mile, go with him two. Give to him who asks of you, and do not turn away from him who wants to borrow from you.

LORD,
I tried turning the other cheek last week and got slapped twice. I usually don't doubt you, but could you be wrong about this? Isn't it better to hit back sometimes? I'm running out of cheeks.

Remember this: Getting even is getting nowhere. Only children take seriously the game of "he hit me first...I did not." Vengeance is the fruit of shoddy forgiveness. How often should we turn the other cheek?

Peter once asked, "How often shall my brother sin against me and I forgive him? Up to seven times?" (Matthew 18:21). Peter seemed to imply there was a limit as to how many times one had to turn the other cheek.

There have been some times in history when cheek turning was the only armament of the dispossessed. At such times, passivity is the only weapon the poor own. Before the hordes of armed aggression, the helpless must sometimes die in numbers sufficient to prevent approaching genocide. This dramatic and suffering tactic of cheek turning has become known as passive resistance.

Will such a tactic work? Can the unarmed win by merely dying? At first, it rarely looks like it. It always appears that the dying are losing. But after a while, killing unarmed people by the thousands can smite the conscience of the most callused. But is this bloody reply an inefficient way to make a point?

Consider the alternative to cheek turning. Can we not sooner get even by returning fire, volley for volley? Will we not establish justice by giving our foes what they deserve? They have plucked out an eye, so now they must lose an eye. Then of course, to really get even they will have to come back to get our remaining eye. Now, blind and chopping at their face, we must go and rip away their final eye. The teeth go next, molar for molar. This is the way warlords play the children's game of "he hit me first...I did not!"

Are you angry with one of your offenders? Forgive the offense seven times. Try the offense of the gospel. Turn the other cheek. Bake your enemy a cake. Did they smash the cake in your face? Develop an appetite for pastries. Take a pie. Out of pies? Write them a celebrative poem exalting their goodness. But never give up cheek turning. You will see. In time...in time...in time.

LORD JESUS,
As you have answered all my sin with grace,
help me to turn to others who need my charity to live.
I will not answer any injustice
with my desire to make them pay.
Rather, help me to reach in love, to give my enemies

more than my foes have ever given me.
I'll turn the cheek—make my forgiveness free!
Amen.

72

MAKING YOUR ENEMIES YOUR NEIGHBORS

MATTHEW 5:43-45

You have heard that it was said, "You shall love your neighbor, and hate your enemy." But I say to you, love your enemies, and pray for those who persecute you in order that you may be sons of your Father who is in heaven; for He causes His sun to rise on the evil and the good, and sends rain on the righteous and the unrighteous.

LORD,
I met a Muslim the other day. All I could think about was that he might be a terrorist. He scared me. He looked funny, and I smiled at him weakly. But the longer we talked, the more Christian and less Islamic he looked. I'm trying to like him, but then there's the little matter of 9-11 and all the Christians who were killed by his kind. His kind are so different from my kind. Is he an enemy? Should I love him?

There are only two categories for most of your relationships: neighbors and enemies! These two different groups earn their labels by living either close to you or farther away. The better you know someone, the easier it is for you to love them and the harder it is for you to hate them. Most of the wars that have destroyed the world might never have happened if the citizens of the opposing nations were forced to take periodic, long vacations within each other's country. It is much easier to hate strangers than acquaintances, and it is nearly impossible for you to want to destroy those you know well.

Why do you give so much grace and unlimited forgiveness to those you know? Why do you reserve ill will for those you do not know? There is a geography in loving, and there is but one solution to keep you from hating your enemies: Move closer to them. Make them your neighbors. The closer they get, the more they will become real people and the harder you will find it is to hate them.

There are three steps you can take to rid your world of enemies.

First, memorize this proverb of proximity: Since it is harder to hate those close at hand, I will allow no strangers in my world. I will seek to move my distant, doubtful acquaintances more and more toward myself.

Second, begin to pray for all of those you are prone to dislike. Such prayers may or may not change the harsh, unlovely qualities of your enemies. But they will change you. After all, the unlovely people that you have called your enemies often have not named you as their enemies. Since you may have misnamed them, why not simply rename them?

Finally, no one can be your enemy until you say so. No one can wear the title of "foe" unless you agree to it. My cross is a great place to remember God has no enemies. He loves everyone exactly as he loves you. And when you are most like God, you will find yourself taking every foe captive by the sheer power of your own generous will.

LORD JESUS,
I have held my own geography too sacred.
I speak to those at hand
and say what I will about those who are more distant.
Now I pray you, help me, in my mind's eye,
to move my distant foes closer.
Help me to see that they, like me, are real.

My foes have their own share of hurt and pain.
I'll love my enemies till we are friends again.
Amen.

73

SECRET GIVING AND OPEN BLESSING

MATTHEW 6:1-4

Beware of practicing your righteousness before men to be noticed by them; otherwise you have no reward with your Father who is in heaven. When therefore you give alms, do not sound a trumpet before you, as the hypocrites do in the synagogues and in the streets, that they may be honored by men. Truly I say to you, they have their reward in full. But when you give alms, do not let your left hand know what your right hand is doing that your alms may be in secret; and your Father who sees in secret will repay you.

LORD, I give quite a bit to good causes. I don't need to be recognized a lot, but it seems like somebody somewhere would mention my sacrifice. I just wish everyone would come to realize that I am a very giving person.

It would amaze you how much you could accomplish in your world if you quit caring who got the credit. Why is it that you want your good works to be noticed? Especially in matters of your church giving. Beware. How ego ever craves the spotlight in the church. Ego often sets in motion a continuing game of one-upmanship in the church. The "how much did *you* give, dearie?" syndrome leads to the most ungodly sorts of competition. In view of my gift on the cross, you would think it would be hard to glory in such ordinary things as church offerings or building pledges. Yet there are only two mystiques for the giver. The first is that of intimate blessing. The second is that of proud exhibitionism. The first hides itself, never disclosing what it has given or why. The second glories in the pronouncement of its generosity. Give discreetly, and you will see that such secrecy causes my Father to become exhibitionist in his blessing.

Selfless giving is the key to his lavish openness.

To tell whether you are giving in the right way, ask yourself who you really love at the moment of your giving. If your focus is only on your gift, the glory you seek will be smudged even as you give. You will only give as the Pharisees once gave. But if you bring your gift to God in silent sacrifice, you will find heaven grows loud in its applause.

Still, never try to hide your love. All real love declares itself with some kind of demonstration. So bring your gift to the altar. But do it in a way that those who watch will focus on me and not your gift. I will then approve your quietly offered gift. It will come wrapped in the simple hush of your own gratitude.

LORD JESUS,
it is so hard for me to want to hide my piety.
It's just that everyone in the church
seems to be playing the game, and it is very hard
not to jump in there and compete.
I want to quit trying to outdo those around me.
Still, I don't want everyone to think I'm a loser.

Help me to give like you gave on the tree
and give my all in anonymity.
Amen.

74

INTIMATE PRAYER

MATTHEW 6:5-6

And when you pray, you are not to be as the hypocrites; for they love to stand and pray in the synagogues and on the street corners, in order to be seen by men. Truly I say to you, they have their reward in full. But you, when you pray, go into your inner room, and when you have shut your door, pray to your Father who is in secret, and your Father who sees in secret will repay you.

LORD,
I hate to admit this, but I love to be asked to say the morning prayers in church. I feel good being up in front of people and praying. I feel so religious. I sure hope you like my public prayers.

Be careful about your spotlight piety. Prayer is supposed to be conversation with my Father. In truth, public prayers are often little more than people talking to each other under the guise of talking to God. Notice the extra volume in public prayer. Hear the dramatic pauses, the swelling images and yes, even gestures. Gestures?

When a man and a woman share in the deepest act of love, it is called intimacy. Intimacy by definition is the loving of two. But if a third person is admitted to the matrix of their loving, the word *intimacy* immediately changes to *obscenity*. So is the definition of spiritual intimacy. Pray in your closet therefore. Then the agony and longings of your heart, the ardor of your spiritual rapture, and your brokenness and need will be heard. The closet is the only place you may be able to tell God everything you are feeling. There, no betrayal is possible. In the closet there is absolutely no possibility that some other human auditor will misunderstand your heart. Only in the closet can you be absolutely sure that the agony and ecstasy of your soul will speak in wordless yearnings that cannot be uttered (Romans 8:26).

The language of such intimacy is of the Spirit. There my Father hears the heart even before it forms the words. Therefore use your closet times with my Father in two ways. First, humble yourself in the silence of your closet while he moves within you—edifying, blessing, rebuking, loving. Your own words will form into praise under the pressure of your inner joy. Second, never feel obligated to bring a large agenda. Come and sit and wait unhurried. Then your petitions will not become larger than your focus on God. Learn the patient discipline of waiting and listening plus nothing— not writing, not words, not forced emotion. Just be there in the closet, taking time for God. Your Father in heaven will visit you, and the visitation will be glorious.

LORD JESUS,
I am afflicted with a busyness
that makes me an infrequent visitor to the prayer closet.
I want to desire you so much
that I find the quiet places in our relationship
altogether welcome.

Meet me when I'm alone and free of fraud,
and ravage me with grace, three-personed God.
Amen.

75

WORDS VS. SILENCE

MATTHEW 6:7-8

And when you are praying, do not use meaningless repetition, as the Gentiles do, for they suppose that they will be heard for their many words. Therefore do not be like them; for your Father knows what you need, before you ask Him.

LORD,
sometimes when I pray, I can't think of very much to say. Still, I want to learn to keep my end of the conversation going.

Your view of praying is what irreverent angels call the blabbermouth syndrome: the notion that the person who prays has to do all the talking while God has to do all the listening. Remember this: At least half of all praying is listening. It is the best half. It is the listening half that allows the Almighty to implant his counsel directly into your life. When the one praying does all the talking, prayer can become little more than presumptuous monologue. Such praying assumes God is mute and only people talk.

There are three rules for keeping an empty "chattiness" out of your praying. First, remember who it is you are praying to. Even most chatty people will get quiet in the presence of true dignity.

A second rule for getting the chattiness out of your praying is to remember to make a distinction between the way you talk and the way you pray. In the whirl and the fury of churchmanship, people often walk into church making conversation. When called upon to pray in the worship service, they go right on talking to God exactly as they have been talking to their friends at church. God receives from them the same chatty tone with which they relate to everyone in their path.

A third rule may indeed eliminate both others. It is an appeal to what the church Fathers called the *otium sanctum*. This *otium sanctum* is translated as "holy leisure." This leisure is the leisure that you should use in approaching God. Leisure is time that is unhurried and unstressed. Leisure is the sort of time you enjoy on vacation. Leisure is different from other kinds of time because it has no agenda that pressures you to produce anything or be concerned about some schedule you must meet.

Consider the way many church people pray. Under the press of all they have to do, they dash in before God's throne. They spill forth the same kind of verbal tornado in which they live. Then having blurted out their agitated prayers, they hurry back into their hurried world, resuming their blustery way of life. To call such frenzied worrying "prayer" is to dishonor prayer.

When you really pray, you must approach God in an unhurried fashion, making a distinct difference from your neurotic agenda. Slow down. Enter his presence in quietness. Garb yourself in unhurried leisure. Say to God, "My time is yours. I have no agenda or schedule more important than you. Speak to me or let me simply enjoy the quiet. I am at leisure. I will abide with you, drinking of your indwelling silence."

LORD JESUS,
I'm often all too noisy
in your presence.
I'm confident that the reason we have two ears
and only one mouth
is that you would like us to listen
twice as much as we talk.
If this is so in life, it ought to be more so in our prayers.

I'm much too present in my chatty prayers.
Let me love silence—then I'll know you're there.
Amen.

76

PRAYING RIGHT

MATTHEW 6:9-15

Pray, then, in this way: "Our Father who art in heaven, Hallowed be Thy name. Thy kingdom come. Thy will be done, On earth as it is in heaven. Gives us this day our daily bread. And forgive us our debts, as we also have forgiven our debtors. And do not lead us into temptation, but deliver us from evil. [For Thine is the kingdom, and the power, and the glory, forever. Amen.]"

For if you forgive men for their transgressions, your heavenly Father will also forgive you. But if you do not forgive men, then your Father will not forgive your transgressions.

LORD, is there really a right and wrong way to pray? I want to do it right, but a conversation with God could hardly ever be wrong whichever course it takes, could it? Can praying in any form ever be wrong?

Beware those prayers that get chatty and spoil themselves. Prayer is more than sanctified gab. If you would pray with power, in every prayer you must do these four things: Hallow my name, pray for my kingdom, thank God for your bread, and forgive everyone as lavishly as I have forgiven you.

First, hallow my name. Be reminded every time you pray that prayer is more than just a conversation between friends. Prayer is the approach of a subject to king. I have taught you throughout the Gospels that God is your Father. Because he is your Father you need never fear to approach him. You may talk to him as friend with friend. But never let your familiarity become so chummy that you see God as a peer. Rather, see him as a great king whose very name is holy. His name, Jehovah, came about as the result of the Jews popularizing Yahweh, the covenant name, so it could be spoken aloud. For ancient Jews had such respect for the holiness of God, they believed it a sin to refer to him aloud by his covenant name, Yahweh. Rejoice that I have brought this holy God near you by becoming a human being just like yourself.

The second thing you should do in your every prayer is pray for my kingdom. I died to establish that kingdom. Day by day for the past 2000 years my kingdom has been adding subjects. Only on that day when I come again will my growing kingdom be complete.

The third thing you should do in your prayers is to thank God daily for your bread. Learn to see that your every provision has come from the generous bounty of my Father. Gratitude to God should always mark your life. Never lift your spoon or your glass without breathing a "thank you" for his gifts.

Finally, let your every prayer be a statement of your praise for his forgiveness. Remember, on my cross I forgave your every sin. You have extravagantly received my cleansing. Now indwelt by this same lavish grace, turn and forgive others whatever they may have done to you.

Let these four axioms undergird your every prayer, for these are the foundations of all prayer. Such prayers will make the world new. To such a world my kingdom will come. In such a world people will hallow my name. Every crust of bread in this kind of world will spawn choruses of praise for the providence of God.

LORD JESUS,
I hallow God's name,
I pray for the coming kingdom,
I thank you for my daily bread,
I forgive lavishly.

I want to pray each day as you have taught,
remembering the price of all you bought.
Amen.

77

SECRET SELF-DENIAL

MATTHEW 6:16
And whenever you fast, do not put on a gloomy face as the
hypocrites do, for they neglect their appearance in order to be seen
fasting by men. Truly I say to you, they have their reward in full.

LORD,
one year I gave up deviled eggs for Lent. I told all my
friends. They were very impressed. The next year I
decided to give up ice cream for Lent, but a half-gallon
of Chocolate Dream ruined my best resolve. I got less
respect than I wanted. I like to give up stuff for God, but
only if I do such a good job I can tell people about it.

There is only one deliverer from all these excesses: self-denial.

Self-denial is not merely a way to hold your mind in check. It serves
your soul too. To say no to any of your appetites is to enter into prayer. Your
prayers put the brakes on these killing indulgences.

You are too overt about your self-denial. The worst form of bondage is
an addiction to a good reputation. Consider the nature of addictions.

The appetites for food, lust, and power can become, among the undisciplined, occasions of continual indulgence. Every addiction to pornogra-
phy rises out of the heart unwilling to check its inner gluttonies. The
addiction to power, which brutalizes in corporations, comes from the
refusal to clear the heart of its addictions. Obesity and alcoholism rise
from other kinds of indulgences.

A similar danger exists in the power appetite. If you secretly desire to
run things, you must hide your desire to control others. You know if your
lust for power becomes obvious, you will be rejected. So in an attempt to
become discreet you become two-souled. You appear to be "one of the regu-
lar guys" always having a good time, but at the same time you are carrying
out your secret agenda of owning others under the pretense of friendship.
If you live this way for too long, you will finally cease to see yourself as you

really are. Your defilement will be so complete that you will continually sin against the race by believing you have a legitimate right to control others.

Finally, consider an appetite that is common among religious people: food. Overeating, however, is a sin often made legitimate within the church. It is the sin "reserved for the pleasure of the godly." Christians rarely bring it up. Gluttony is a rare sermon topic among those who constantly run to church casserole suppers and ice-cream parties. But every overindulgence should be a matter of conscience. Make nothing legitimate that has the power to control you. Deny yourself. Live free. Surrender every bad habit you own before it owns you.

LORD JESUS,
I want to be as I appear,
for I know that sham is the number one accusation
against those who are in the church.

No one will hear a thing I really have to say
while I remain so squarely in the way.
Amen.

78

TAKE OFF YOUR MASK

MATTHEW 6:17-18

But you, when you fast, anoint your head, and wash your face so that you may not be seen fasting by men, but by your Father who is in secret; and your Father who sees in secret will repay you.

LORD,
I don't mind telling my friends at church how much I do for Jesus. I tell them all the time, but they don't seem to look very interested. Why are people so disinterested in my sacrifice?

Doing good is better done when the doer hasn't noticed he did it. The Pharisees were inclined to remind the less good people how very good they were. They fasted to God but went around trying to look as starved as they possibly could so the whole world would remember how sacrificial they were.

I encourage you to fast too. After all, gluttony shortens life. But remember, your conquering of this common passion requires the same submission of ego as the management of any of your other sins. Fasting is a good way to rule over appetite. Still, as I reminded the hypocrites of my day, you must not allow any form of self-denial to propel you into the center of community esteem. If you fast only in order to advance a godly reputation, you have only denied your food appetite to indulge your power appetite.

Whatever your form of self-denial, keep it to yourself. Deliver your needs to my Father. Begin to talk to him in secret about them. Make a silent pact between the two of you.

The Pharisees fasted so regularly they never really came to know God. When they fasted, they worked hard to let it show! They didn't shave or wash their long, long faces. Their hair was disheveled. Their complexions wan. They looked dour. All who looked at them were prone to say, "My, what godly men! See, it is clear! They fast!" Others saw them and wondered, *Who wants to be religious if it hurts so much?*

The English word for *hypocrite* comes from the Greek word *hupocrites,*

159

which refers to an actor's mask. Acting can become such a group preoccupation in some churches that rarely is anyone whom he appears to be. Many are playing "dress up" to conceal their need or cloak their private agendas. Seek out some old-fashioned gathering in which you are free to bring your masks and lay them on the altar. Even as you walk away from such old, false faces, a better kind of power will be born within you. When you have become a naked-faced believer, my power will live in you. I will be your God; you will be my disciple. Pretense will be gone.

LORD JESUS,
a dozen times each day
I put on some mask
that in my heart I believe will
entice others to fuss over me.

I need an unmasked entry into grace,
a way to follow with a naked face.
Amen.

79

MOTH AND RUST

MATTHEW 6:19-21

Do not lay up for yourselves treasures upon earth, where moth and rust destroy, and where thieves break in and steal. But lay up for yourselves treasures in heaven, where neither moth nor rust destroys, and where thieves do not break in or steal; for where your treasure is, there will your heart be also.

LORD,
I believe in heaven, but I've got a long way to go till I get there. I'm saving up for the golden years so I'll have enough "gold" to last through them. I like sockin' it away. It gives me the feeling of getting somewhere. I'm becoming self-sufficient. I'm self-made. Nobody will have to worry about me. I'm saving up to take care of myself.

Save, but do not become a slave to your bounty. I have two words I'm sending to be your bedfellows. The words are *moth* and *rust.* Moth and rust are cancers on endurance. One devours steel, the other cloth. Rust eats all metal: crowns, thrones, military hardware. Moths do their work in the dank closets of our self-importance. The velvet and ermine of regal dress yield at last to the appetites of common insects.

In safety-deposit boxes and hotel vaults are the registered collections of things we would weep to lose. I must ask you this: What would you weep to lose? What do you own that is so dear that you would shrink from every thought of misplacing it?

There is also a vault in heaven to which I invite your attention! It glitters with true wealth. Here, in these endless ranks of eternal safety-deposit boxes, lie the enduring things, which neither rust nor moths could destroy. Here in heaven are kept the flaming stakes of martyrs who deposited their unyielding commitment to truth. Here the reformers laid the treasure of their courage. But really, the best treasures of heaven are not historically grand. Here are kept the tears of a child, suffering from the quarrels of her divorcing parents. Here lies the steadfast soul of a minister abused by wealthy parishioners. Here the dying inmate laid his years of crying in the dark, where none could see. Here in this vault, the thief on the cross, criminal that he was, laid down his fleeting life to take it up as jewels in another world. Here Magdalene wept out her need for full forgiveness, and the glittering rubies of her repentance were safely stored to be opened in better times.

You will see plenty of rust during your lifetime. Moths will be frequent. Therefore do not store up treasure on earth. You are the treasure to my Father. Treasure him, and heaven will become the reading of your splendid will. You are the heir to this glittering testament.

LORD JESUS,
there is but one kind of valuable.
There is but one place to store my valuables.
In the vaults of heaven,
where all the best treasures are kept,
there are glittering shelves
of simple things;
virtue, self-sacrifice, commitment.

I want to lay up treasures all untold,
those things that never can be bought with gold.
Amen.

80

NO STRANGLING LILY, NO WORRIED BIRD

MATTHEW 6:25-33

For this reason I say to you, do not be anxious for your life, as to what you shall eat, or what you shall drink; nor for your body, as to what you shall put on. Is not life more than food and the body than clothing? Look at the birds of the air, that they do not sow, neither do they reap, nor gather into barns, and yet your heavenly Father feeds them. Are you not worth much more than they? And which of you by being anxious can add a single cubit to his life's span? And why are you anxious about clothing? Observe how the lilies of the field grow; they do not toil nor do they spin, yet I say to you that even Solomon in all his glory did not clothe himself like one of these. But if God so arrays the grass of the field, which is alive today and tomorrow is thrown into the furnace, will He not much more do so for you, O men of little faith? Do not be anxious then, saying, "What shall we eat?" or "What shall we drink?" or "With what shall we clothe ourselves?" For all these things the Gentiles eagerly seek; for your heavenly Father knows that you need all these things. But seek first His kingdom and His righteousness; and all these things shall be added to you.

LORD,
I have been told by some very busy people that I have a very busy lifestyle. I have been told by two or three champions of the hassle that I appear to them to be very hassled. I want to be a person of peace, and yet I have so much going on. So many things to do that I am sometimes frantic. But busy people are happy people.

Remember that I am the Christ of the lilies and birds. I offer their hassle-free existence to you as a metaphor of peace. Remember them and give anxiety no place in your life. Your worries and anxieties only distract your focus from all things important. Focus on what matters, and trivial things will take a lesser place. The mind is a very narrow channel. It permits us to think of only one thing at a time. A single mind does not have enough room for purposeful thinking and trivial self-concern to sit together. On what trivia do you focus? Which functions shall you attend? What shall you eat when you get there? Can you eat that much and stay on your diet? If you eat the main course, can you really eat those fatty desserts and heavy entrees? If you don't eat, will you appear ungracious or as though you are living in judgment on those who do?

If a simple dinner invitation can engender so many questions, consider the anxieties you feel around the issue of clothes. Many spend their lives buying clothes, washing clothes, putting them on, primping before mirrors, and receiving the compliments. So you spend yourself to look just right for that just right occasion. The formal event, the wedding, the funeral, or the governor's reception. Your concerns leave you paralyzed.

While your mind swelters in issues of eating or dressing right, the flowers go on blanketing the hillsides. Effortlessly they grow.

Remember the flowers and put to death all those cares and concerns that have been strangling you for years. Remember this: The word *anxiety* comes from an old Latin word *angere,* which means "to strangle or to choke," and the word *worry* comes from another ancient word, *wyrgan,* which also means "to strangle or to choke." Worry and anxiety strangle the single focus. But on the other hand, a single focus on the kingdom will strangle worry and anxiety. The recipe for personal peace is simple. Be like the wildflowers. Think *only* about what God wants. Take a day off. The lilies are growing. The birds are singing. God is in charge.

LORD JESUS,
Let me see the wildflowers in December,
for it's then I have the hardest time remembering
that you naturally clothe the world in beauty.

Let those things that choke and strangle me
remind me where my focus ought to be.
Amen.

81

TODAY IS THE ONLY ERA IN WHICH YOU MAY LIVE

MATTHEW 6:34

Therefore do not be anxious for tomorrow; for tomorrow will care for itself. Each day has enough trouble of its own.

LORD,
I'm concerned about the future. I guess it's where I'm headed. But life is unsure, and there is no such thing as security. What shall I do? How can I make sure tomorrow is safe and all that I need will be in place when I get there?

To live only for today is foolish, for eternity is long. But if you are so consumed by future fear that you cannot make the moment meaningful, you are equally foolish. You cannot live in tomorrow. It is a locked land. Its walls are high. Futurology is the science of warlocks.

There is but one way to get ready for tomorrow. Live today, for today is the porch of tomorrow. Then ask yourself, *What is this present moment really for?* It is a place for meeting God. You cannot unravel the past, wishing you had met God more frequently back there. Nor can you stalk him in your tomorrow. If you would know him at all, today is all the time you have.

Embrace the *now*. It is glorious. *Now* is the only address you can fully own. Only in the present moment can you sow tomorrow's harvest. Plant what you will, or let it lay fallow with dreaming. You may conquer any bad habit only in the present land of *now*. Only here can you apologize to a wounded ally and restore a golden friendship.

The gold you crave lies only in today.

LORD JESUS,
I have wasted so much of my life
worrying about problems that never came.
I have counted on the mine I thought I would discover,
so much so that I never saw the gold about my feet.

I want today to be defined by grace
and let tomorrow keep its proper place.
Amen.

82

HOW DO YOU LIKE THAT?

MATTHEW 7:1-2
Do not judge lest you be judged. For in the way you judge, you will be judged; and by your standard of measure, it will be measured to you.

LORD,
it is hard to separate the need to be a critical thinker from actually becoming a nasty critic. I don't want to be judgmental, and yet I want to be a person of sound judgment. How can I become a good judge of evil without becoming evil in my judgment?

Have your ever heard vindictive children fighting? With his little fist, one child will strike the other and say, "How do you like that?" The other, not to be outdone, will double up his little fist and strike back crying, "And how do you like that?"

For many this game persists through life. From childhood you were taught not to let anyone get the best of you. More than that, you were taught that to stay on top you must get the best of others. The older you grew, the less prone you were to hurt others with your fists. You learned to slash back with judgment and gossip.

During medieval times, gossip was often called "regathering feathers." In those days pillows were stuffed with feathers. Gossip was seen as taking one of those feather pillows to the steeple of the church and ripping it open. As those tiny feathers settled over the entire community, the villagers could see that they could never be regathered again.

So it is with hasty judgments. You can never regather all your "How do you like that?" comments. Do not hide behind the cliché that "sticks and stones can break the bones, but words can never hurt you." How false! Words can hurt the most. Your words can destroy the self-respect of others and cut into the soft, tender well-being of those we disrespect. Sticks and stones can only bruise outwardly, but words excise the heart and leave the life shattered for years.

Never judge?

Will judging others ever make you feel better about yourself? In cutting others down, can you really rise in your own gloating self-esteem? No. It is a sad and spurious self-esteem you try to gain by judging others.

There is a better recipe for feeling good about yourself. Love those you would like to judge. When you affirm others, a wonderful therapy also begins to heal your own critical spirit. Instead of seeing the faults of others, you begin to see your own. Your own belligerence finds grace. Love replaces censure.

LORD JESUS,
I give up this foolish game of one-upmanship.
"How do you like that?" is not an appropriate game for those
who've seen the cross.

I cannot measure others as their judge
when you have come to heal my caustic grudge.
Amen.

83

ABUNDANCE

LUKE 6:38

Give, and it will be given to you; good measure, pressed down, shaken together, running over, they will pour into your lap. For by your standard of measure it will be measured to you in return.

LORD,
when I have given, can I expect you to give to me in return? Is there some universal principle of grand return? Is God ample in his generosity? Does he see the trifle my poverty affords and set my little gift against his grand coffers in heaven?

As you give you will be blessed. Earth's shabbiest banking is done by stingy disciples whose grudging mathematics are pried from their unwilling purses.

One grand truth lies behind the banking of the heart. God ordained people to be happy only when they were willing to become channels of wealth and not strongboxes of ego. How many millionaires have you known who wrote books on the meaningful life? Probably not many. For most millionaires, meaning consists only in how much they own. Yet happiness, like meaning, often eludes then. They aren't always happy with what they have because it only reminds them of how much they still do not possess. Ask any millionaire how many dollars it would take to make him truly happy, and he will likely answer, "Just one more."

So those who appear to have all often have nothing. They feel as if they never have quite enough. Those missionaries who serve in the poorer countries of the world have experienced a glorious phenomenon. They must be very careful when giving materially to the poor members of their flock. For if they add to some poor family's single possession of worth, the family will likely give back that sole treasure.

What's a missionary to do? To receive this single, prized possession seems to completely disinherit their impoverished benefactors. Still, the only way for the poor to feel rich is to see themselves as a channel of wealth.

Do you want real treasure? Give till you feel wealthy. To feel really rich, you may have to give a lot.

Remember Good Friday. All I owned was taken away. Even my coat became the sport of gamblers. Some say I died naked and bereft. Nonsense! What I really owned was being held on deposit just a world away. I had given everything to gain the treasure I sought most: my Father's pleasure.

Do you want such treasure? Then rehearse the art of giving. Use the biggest scoop you can find to shovel your resources into the treasury of God. For whatever you use to shovel your substance into God's treasury, you may be sure his shovel will make yours seem like a thimble. For his riches are great, and his desire is to give it all to his children.

LORD JESUS,
I do not want to save and scrimp my way
to utter poverty of soul.
I'd rather teach my world that to have everything
is to give it all away.
Only what I keep will make me poor.

Here! Take my lean account of poverty.
I trade it all for heaven's currency.
Amen.

84

HOLY OPHTHALMOLOGY

MATTHEW 7:3-5

And why do you look at the speck that is in your brother's eye, but do not notice the log that is in your own eye? Or how can you say to your brother, "Let me take the speck out of your eye," and behold, the log is in your own eye? You hypocrite, first take the log out of your own eye, and then you will see clearly to take the speck out of your brother's eye.

LORD, the thing I hate most about my critical spirit is that it presumes that I am superior in character to those I criticize. Help me understand that I lack any real perfection of soul that gives me the right to judge others.

A critical spirit is a blind guide. Leave it out of your life.

Once a blind man, having a heavy schedule for the day, rose early. He had gotten dressed so quickly that when he stepped out into the morning commerce he still had his comb sticking in his hair. As he walked through his world, he began to condemn the loud talk of the people around him. He congratulated himself that he was not as ill-tempered as the quarrelsome hagglers in the marketplace. He felt good in his heart that he was not as boisterous as those who pushed and elbowed their way around him. He enjoyed feeling superior to those he secretly condemned.

While he thus gloried in his own intellectual superiority, he ran his hand across his hair to discover, with horror, that he had left his comb in his hair when he had gotten dressed to go to work. He was suddenly washed with healthy shame. It is dangerous to try to pick the speck out of other's eyes with the logs of condemnation in your own.

Let's talk about healthy shame. Healthy shame is not that which you seek to project on others, making them feel guilty because they lack your excellence. Healthy shame is that which you inflict on yourself. The sweetest words in the ears of our heavenly Father are these: "O God, forgive me for presuming I was so much more than I really am!"

Remember the tale of the elegant church lady who had a louse on her hat? In her own mind, she was the very picture of cultural refinement. In her icy sophistication, she presumed herself queen of all the underlings in her religious world. Her presumption held no mercy for the unsophisticated. But a small insect—vile and unacceptable—cavorting on the brim of her ego, eradicated her right to judge.

So be careful in your practice of Christian ophthalmology. Blind ophthalmologists can complicate the saving work of God. It takes a really good eye to see what's wrong with a bad one.

LORD JESUS,
I must confess the sin
of trying to help others see
when I myself can't read your eye chart.
How arrogant I have been
in presuming my vision clear enough
to prescribe sight for others.

Wash my clouded vision with an honest mind,
And give me grace to see I too am blind.
Amen.

85

OF PIGS AND PEARLS

MATTHEW 7:6
Do not give what is holy to dogs, and do not throw your pearls
before swine, lest they trample them under their feet, and turn and
tear you to pieces.

LORD,
I spoke of you today to a very intelligent man, but he
simply chuckled at my childlike trust and then explained
why the things I believe cannot possibly be true. I felt as
if he had dragged your name through the mud, as if he
had casually tossed away my most treasured possession.
It hurt to see him treat you so poorly, so casually. I felt
devalued too.

Remember this: Hogs are not good at values. A pig sty is a poor place
to have your pearls evaluated. Understand spiritual values for what they
are. Many is the young college woman who, entering the instruction of an
avant-garde professor, must listen while the worldly-wise philosopher
shreds her Christian worldviews. She then leaves class emotionally
destroyed. All that she learned to cherish in church has been dragged
through the sloughs of academic logic. She weeps in shame that she has no
answers to offer the intellectual assassins of her faith.

Further, she remembers her parents and how they too believed all that
the professor has scoffed at. Now she must also despise what her parents
have taught her. Her mind gathers its hurt against her parent's naïveté. How
could they have believed such simple, unproveable doctrines? How could
they have taught her such nonsense?

What can regather such a heart? What will put humpty-dumpty back
together again? There is but one great doctrine. Keep your pearls out of pig
pens. Pigs do not esteem elegance. Swine are not jewelers. Feel only pity for
those who try to make the great mysteries of faith perform for tiny poly-
graphs. Mystery rarely explains itself in the halls of logic.

Do not misunderstand me, scholars are not pigs in the sense of their worth to God. God loves atheists with the same ardor that he loves believers. But scholars may be pigs in the sense that their value system has not esteemed the mystery of godliness. A pig's chief crime is not that it doesn't recognize the wealth of pearls but that it is addicted to its love of the sty. Pigs are by nature pigs. They cannot transcend their piggyness to contemplate beauty and meaning. Every pig has a narrow focus that never moves beyond loving the mire that cools it and the swill that makes it fat. Academic atheists too have stayed too long within the confining boundaries of their little sciences to see those realities their science cannot measure.

Truth is vast, and nobody's a specialist at everything. A janitor who prays may be a better person to teach you about faith than a physicist who doesn't. A doubting biologist may be less a specialist on the mystery of godliness than a praying child. Your pearls are your faith. Never hand them over to those who neither understand nor treasure them.

LORD JESUS,
I want to meet the atheist who challenges me
and my faith
as someone whose knowledge only qualifies him to speak narrowly.
I want never to forget he may be too focused on academic logic
to have the whole picture.

And old men who have prayed through pain and night
are scholars with another kind of light.
Amen.

86

TRUTH HUNGER

MATTHEW 7:7-8

Ask, and it shall be given to you; seek, and you shall find; knock, and it shall be opened to you. For everyone who asks receives, and he who seeks finds, and to him who knocks it shall be opened.

LORD,
I seek you. Even when you seem so far away. I seek you as one who is desperate for the finding. Bless me as I seek.

You are blessed indeed. Seeking speaks of the ardor in your faith. Seeking is the calling that heaven calls the glory of humanity. Only one appetite supremely matters: seeking after God. Only one human sin is eternally damning: not seeking after God. The apostle Paul wrote these words:

The wrath of God is being revealed from heaven against all the godlessness and wickedness of men who suppress the truth by their wickedness, since what may be known about God is plain to them, because God has made it plain to them. For since the creation of the world God's invisible qualities—his eternal power and divine nature—have been clearly seen, being understood from what has been made, so that men are without excuse (Romans 1:18-20 NIV).

Do not think the apostle too harsh. Those ignorant of God commit the same sin as those who know him. It is not the sin of being ignorant that condemns humankind before the throne of God. It's the sin of being content in ignorance.

The sin of those who know me is the same sin of those who don't. It is the sin of the lost not to seek to understand more about the God they do not know. It is the chief sin of the saved not to want to understand more about the God they do know. The ignorant, according to the apostle, are not damned because of their ignorance. They do know some things. They can look around and see that the world has been made by a Creator. Seeing the little and the obvious, they sin by not wanting to know more about God. So both the saved and the lost sin the same sin. They are too content with their partial knowledge.

To live content in ignorance is not the unforgivable sin; it is just the unthinkable sin. The world perishes not because grace is in short supply but because it considers grace of no real importance.

Come to God to abandon your willful ignorance.

Come to God asking. He has answers that will turn your questions into doorways of everlasting truth.

Come to him seeking. He will not hide himself. He will stand in the open light of heaven to disclose the relationship you hunger for.

Come knocking. He is standing at the door, eager to open it and fold you into the glory of his presence.

Come to God hungry to know me, find me, and enter my embrace. Such simple hungers wake the angels to dancing. Hurry then to light! Ask. Seek. Knock.

LORD JESUS,
Do you hear my feeble knocking?
I have always knocked too slightly,
afraid I would wake God from his napping
and find him irritated with me.
Oh, may I delight him by my eager knocking.

I'll loudly rap, create a noisy din,
to hear my lover cry, "My child, come in!"
Amen.

87

THE GOLDEN RULE

MATTHEW 7:12
Therefore, however you want people to treat you, so treat them, for
this is the Law and the Prophets.

LORD,
I want to care about others, but who's to care about me?
Tell me again of heaven's remedy! Does it really stop all
pain?

All you have to do is figure out how you want the world to treat you and
then grant the world the kindness you desire it to give to you. As it has been
well said, "If the mothers of the world were allowed to plan the battles, all
wars would cease." Most of the pain inflicted on the weeping is ordered by
people who have no pain. The depraved evils of the Inquisition were
ordered by healthy priests. Burning witches is only fun when you hold the
matches. Sadism is enjoyed only by well-fed torturers who are getting a
warm bath and a neck rub every night.

Once in a land ruled by a tyrant, a young field worker committed an
indiscretion during a state harvest. The boy had stolen a handful of grain
for his starving parents. When he was caught, he was sentenced to die in a
small bamboo cage. In this cage he could neither comfortably stand nor lie
down. Cramped into this fetal position he died, whimpering for water and
covered with ants and his own excrement. Death was the only mercy he
could pray for. His weeping parents, for whom he had stolen the grain,
looked on from a distance, praying for him to die.

Would you like to understand the true meaning of the golden rule?
Don't seek an ethicist to explain its high morality. Study the injustices that
others bring upon you. Celebrate that pain. Only as you suffer from pain
will you learn the Golden Rule. Then you will not nurture vengeance so
that you may someday get even. Your hurt will teach you a generosity of
spirit. You will determine never to be that kind of person. You will resolve
never to inflict on anyone else what you have suffered.

To the suffering parents of the youth who stole grain to save them, I offer only my own mother's understanding. She, like them, once watched me die. She felt the sword that Simeon predicted 30 years earlier. Her suffering at the cross pierced her own soul through (Luke 2:35). Ah, poor suffering parents, it is the pierced that understand the piercing. It is only the wronged who know how grievous wrong really is.

Let hurt be your teacher. Let what others have done to you cause you to pledge with honest tears: I will never, never, never do that to another.

LORD JESUS,
let me live in continual rehearsal
of those hurts I've felt at others' hands,
not to get even with the world
but so that my memory will make me be an agent of gentle love.

I prize the scars from conflicts I've not won
and pledge: No wounds like mine to anyone.
Amen.

88

TWO ROADS

MATTHEW 7:13-14

Enter by the narrow gate; for the gate is wide, and the way is broad
that leads to destruction, and many are those who enter by it. For
the gate is small, and the way is narrow that leads to life, and few
are those who find it.

LORD,
it's dark tonight. I've lost the way, I think. I have no light,
yet I beg light. Set my feet upon the way.

You need not have another point you to the way. To hunger for the way
is to own the way. No one ever missed the way—even in the deepest night—
if he hungered for the way.

You can easily tell if you're on the road to heaven. That way is never
crowded. The broad road to hell, on the other hand, is full of people and
marked with the spirit of a parade.

Rehearse the way of discipline. The word *disciple* and the word *discipline* are forms of the same word. Grace is God's gift to you, but your gift
to him is discipline. Grace, being God's part, is easy for you, while it cost
God everything. I came to earth and died to pay the price for your salvation. Grace, like any gift, is free to you, the receiver. But oh, how such gifts
cost the giver!

Discipline is your gift to God because all the prayer, ministry, and sacrifice you give him comes from your own desire. God will never put a revolver
to your head and order you to pray, read the Bible, or minister to others. If
you ever do these things, they will come from your overwhelming desire to
please God.

Many are prone to sing "Amazing Grace," but few have the honesty to
sing "Amazing Discipline." Yet it is discipline that is truly amazing, for disciplined believers are hard to find. They are rare as diamonds. They are
diamonds.

Apart from the size of the crowd on the road, you hold one other infallible guide to distinguishing the roads between heaven and hell. The road to heaven is rigorous and requiring. The discipline of holiness causes the road to rise in steep ascent. The broad road that leads elsewhere is comfortably wide and gradual in its descent. If you are in a company of those who feel no obligation to celebrate the disciplines, you may be sure you are not on the road to heaven. On the road to heaven, you will feel the obligation to minister, pray, study, and worship.

But these demanding activities are not torturous. They are disciplines of joy. No true believer complains about these disciplines. They rejoice that their burden is light. They crave heaven's compliment: "Well done."

So come to the upper road. The altitude is glorious. Here and there the mists roll back enough to let you see the towers of heaven through undiluted light.

LORD JESUS,
conversion is that fork where routes divide.
I'm glad I took the road less traveled.
For the journey is direct
to the only place where I can live forever.

I bask in golden light and thinner air;
I see sometimes that city built foursquare.
Amen.

THE ART OF FRUIT
INSPECTING

Beware of false prophets, who come to you in sheep's clothing, but
inwardly are ravenous wolves. You will know them by their fruits.
Grapes are not gathered from thorn bushes, nor figs from thistles,
are they? Even so, every good tree bears good fruit; but the bad
tree bears bad fruit. A good tree cannot produce bad fruit, nor can
a bad tree produce good fruit. Every tree that does not bear good
fruit is cut down and thrown into the fire. So then, you will know
them by their fruits.

LORD,
tell me that the product that issues from my life is
enough to let the world know that I am your follower.
Is it enough? Is it?

It is often said in ruse that Christians are not permitted to be judges,
only fruit inspectors. There is some truth in this skewed proverb. How are
a judge and a fruit inspector different? A judge makes rulings and offers
stern sentences and reprimands of redress. A fruit inspector merely
acknowledges that the quality of the fruit passes or fails.

There is no Christianity without values. Some of your deeds are bad
and some good. Some things you do are sinful and some not. There is a
clear right and a clear wrong. Some things are always wrong, and others
are always right. Some values are always bad, and others are always good.
God gave his Ten Commandments to furnish you a guide to fruit inspecting. God's values are constant from generation to generation, century to
century, millennium to millennium.

It has been well said that you are what you eat. If you sample the illicit
or the lurid, you will become what you eat. The key is all in your diet. Never
taste what you do not want to become.

Then there will be fruit—good fruit born of a good tree. You will be

that tree, and what you produce will be beautiful and usable by all who
have the good fortune to touch your life.

LORD JESUS,
knowing right from wrong is not the hard part.
It is eating what I know is good for me that seems so difficult to do.
I want to please you by distinguishing right from wrong.
I want to ingest only that which I know is good for me.

This is the feast the hungry heart knows best:
the wondrous, holy fruit of righteousness.
Amen.

90

SAYING THE WORD AND MEANING WHAT YOU SAY

MATTHEW 7:21-23

Not everyone who says to Me, "Lord, Lord," will enter the kingdom of heaven; but he who does the will of My Father who is in heaven. Many will say to Me on that day, "Lord, Lord, did we not prophesy in Your name, and in Your name cast out demons, and in Your name perform many miracles?" And then I will declare to them, "I never knew you; depart from Me, you who practice lawlessness."

LORD,
I call you Lord because it's who you are. It implies a lot of things about me to call you that, but one thing it makes clear is this: If you are my Lord, then I can't be. Confused people only *refer* to you as Lord while they go on managing their affairs and planning their lives. May I always call you Lord and mean what I call you.

You have reached for a noble goal. Heaven is not achieved by chanting a mantra. There are no special deeds that will achieve heaven. Even ministry to the sick or the imprisoned will not. There are those who have performed such wonderful deeds in the name of social agencies or service clubs.

Heaven knows only one language that will open the gates. It is the language of relationship. Eternity opens only to those whose confidence lies in their longing. Those who run through the high gates with open arms are welcome. These don't need to be celebrated for the ministry they once gave God. Their need recommends them. They must go to heaven, for they are unfulfilled without God. They have never sought heaven as a way out of the maze of their lower choices. These see heaven as the dwelling place of God and the only place they would ever want to live.

Those who call me Lord to flatter me would find heaven too up-front for their liking. On the contrary, those who call me Lord out of utter need will be welcome in heaven forever. Those who have ministered in my name will of course find heaven a delightful place to live. Those who did good deeds for any other reason would find heaven too void of self-interest to appeal to them.

Some people spend their lives doing good things for bad reasons. They want people to fuss over them for their heroic and showy goodness. These people would find heaven unattractive, for heaven is not a place where arrogance goes on admiring itself.

Heaven is really for those who saw a needy world and agreed to be my hands and feet in ministry. These have but to whisper my name, and the angels will come to attention; the gates will swing wide.

LORD JESUS,
when I say, "Lord," help me to mean
"I love you."
When I tell anyone of the good I've done,
help me to say,
"It is for him alone my life holds any merit."

I want to live my life so every word
sounds like a choral anthem to my Lord.
Amen.

91

MAKING THE WISDOM OF CHRIST LIFE'S FOUNDATION

MATTHEW 7:24-27
Therefore everyone who hears these words of Mine, and acts upon them, may be compared to a wise man, who built his house upon the rock. And the rain descended, and the floods came, and the winds blew, and burst against that house; and yet it did not fall, for it had been founded upon the rock. And everyone who hears these words of Mine, and does not act upon them, will be like a foolish man, who built his house upon the sand. And the rain descended, and the floods came, and the winds blew, and burst against that house; and it fell, and great was its fall.

LORD,
I want to be a person of conviction, like Martin Luther. I want to cry, "Here I stand," but only if where I stand is not the crust of quicksand. Help me to stand on firm ground and care about the solid ground of rock-hard truth.

You have desired the only kind of soil secure enough to anchor the solid life. No building or life is more secure than its foundation. When the great cathedrals were built, their transepts often rose 14 stories above the cathedral floor. The buildings took centuries to complete. Only the distant descendants of those who began the church ever saw it brought to completion. A whole generation of foundation building was required before the superstructure of the church was ever started. Some foundations required 80 years to build. The builders wanted to be sure the foundations went down far enough into the ground to support walls and roofs that would not be complete for five more centuries. Those who laid the foundations gave their entire lifetimes to be sure that those who inherited their dream could go on building in confidence.

To be sure, it is more exhilarating to set the capstone on a spire 800 years later. It is always more fulfilling to cry, "It is finished" than "It has begun." Still, if those who laid the foundations did not take their work seriously, there would have been no finishing cry.

Do you love to worship me? Do you find great exhilaration in singing my praise? Praise is the pinnacle work of the Christian life. But do not despise the foundational work of discipleship.

Without foundations, all the exhilaration of your private worship and praise will be a soil too spongy on which to build the later, higher towers of adoration. In joyous worship you must lay the foundations of your faith well, for the cosmic tides of secularism will soon pound against them. The gales of unbelief will try to erode your confidence. The sand beneath all undisciplined holiness dissolves. You can only enjoy the exalting work of praise after you have faced the requiring work of strong foundations.

Dig down into the soul with the spade of Bible reading and prayer. Then pour the steely strata of studied endurance under your frail life. Reinforce your foundling hopes with the iron rods of discipline. Then will the tower of joyous praise rise above the strong foundations of your inner life. Then will the world look at you and see me.

LORD JESUS,
I want to be sure
I base my towering dreams
upon deep and secure foundations.
Help me see that
my life can only reach the heights
as your power reaches down,
making certain the piers of my insecurity.

I have set my dreams upon a solid stand,
a granite pier in fickle, shifting sand.
Amen.

92

GOD HAS VISITED HIS PEOPLE

LUKE 7:11-17

And it came about soon afterwards, that He went to a city called Nain; and His disciples were going along with Him, accompanied by a large multitude. Now as He approached the gate of the city, behold, a dead man was being carried out, the only son of his mother, and she was a widow; and a sizable crowd from the city was with her. And when the Lord saw her, He felt compassion for her, and said to her, "Do not weep." And He came up and touched the coffin; and the bearers came to a halt. And He said, "Young man, I say to you, arise!" And the dead man sat up, and began to speak. And Jesus gave him back to his mother. And fear gripped them all, and they began glorifying God, saying, "A great prophet has arisen among us!" and, "God has visited His people!" And this report concerning Him went out all over Judea, and in all the surrounding district.

LORD, I have a friend who lost a child. The burden was a grief none could allay. Tell me how to counsel such a loss. Is there enough consolation in this despair to make the loss seem reasonable or meaningful? Can all dying have some reason? Some significance?

Have you ever wept because of loss? I tell you this: You did not weep alone. My Father cries when you cry. Human grief is intolerable for God. He hurts when his children hurt. Heaven is set against all crying. There my Father will at last wipe away all tears.

I was torn by the grief of the little woman I saw one day in the little town of Nain. Bent by despair, she followed the coffin of her son. Her shoulders were rounded, heaving with the convulsions of her brokenness. Her pain stabbed at me with compassion. She had already wept at the grave of her husband. Now she must grieve again.

I acted.

I had the power to do it, for God holds the power of life, and I am his only begotten Son. It was easy for me to say, "Young man, I say to you, arise!" He did.

How odd to see a corpse sit up, surrendering his stillness. He stared, blinking into the sunlight to make his eyes adjust. He smiled. That smile sent chills down the spines of all who followed the coffin. They gasped in fear. The uncanny event froze the morrow and raised the hair on the neck.

Their fear gave way to wonder as he swung his legs over the side of the coffin and stepped down onto the ground. Their awe was swallowed up in joy and wild applause as he approached his mother. The deadness in her grief came suddenly alive. A great gift had been given to her.

Someone cried, "God has visited his people!" Rejoicing broke out around the miracle. Grief had taken off its muddy boots, and human joy danced cleanly in the streets.

Have you grieved? Are you now in grief? Remember that you are not alone. God loves a broken heart. Someday he will say to the loved one you have lost, "Arise." For everyone over whom you've cried will one day be restored to you. And God will wipe away all tears, and you will sing throughout the endless years of eternity, "Indeed, God has visited his people."

LORD JESUS,
I have wept at many gravesides,
yet because of your victory,
I've never had to sorrow
as those who have no hope.
Someday I'll be in stillness
and wait for you to speak to those long dead.
Then wake me
unto life eternal.

I cannot wait till I caress the skies,
in hearing you command, "I've come! Arise!"
Amen.

93

ARE YOU HE?

LUKE 7:18-23

And the disciples of John reported to him about all these things. And summoning two of his disciples, John sent them to the Lord, saying, "Are You the Expected One, or do we look for someone else?" And when the men had come to Him, they said, "John the Baptist has sent us to You, saying, "Are You the Expected One, or do we look for someone else?" At that very time He cured many people of diseases and afflictions and evil spirits; and He granted sight to many who were blind. And He answered and said to them, "Go and report to John what you have seen and heard: the blind receive sight, the lame walk, the lepers are cleansed, and the deaf hear, the dead are raised up, the poor have the gospel preached to them. And blessed is he who keeps from stumbling over Me."

LORD,
I have to pray so often, "I believe, Lord; help my unbelief." We all stake so much on believing...no wonder it seems we are prone to doubt from time to time. Is it a sin to wonder if you really are the Christ, and if you are, why do I find myself so often in doubt about it?

Doubt is not sin. It is sometimes the honest examination of an idea too wonderful to seem real. There is only one way to determine if I am the Christ. You must dredge the answer from your heart. It is true for you; it was true for John. John was a man who knew why he was in the world. He knew he existed for only one reason: to announce the kingdom. I was the reason John came. Perhaps in the prison, John began to sense he would never get out. In the loneliness of his cell he wondered, doubted, and questioned. "What if? What if this Jesus is not the Christ? What if I am forever locked away and cannot serve that cause for which I was born? If Jesus is not the Christ, and I never get out of this prison...what has been the purpose of my life?"

So John sent his disciples to ask, "Are you he?" He knew, of course, the question could only be answered either yes or no. I was the true Christ, but I could not convince him with a mere "Yes sir, I am! I would swear it on a stack of Torahs!" I knew I could not answer this question for John. This question John must answer for himself. My being the Christ is the faith question that none can answer for another. Each person must believe or disbelieve, find or lose the affirmation within his or her own soul.

"Are you he?"

I answered John the only way I could, "Look around you, John. See what may be seen and then decide yourself. Wherever I pass, I leave the cold dead world in a state of resurrection. The crippled run. The mute are singing. The dead are spoiling the dignity of their funerals by leaping from their caskets. The poor, who rarely get any good news, have the good news preached to them regularly. Prisoners are free. Joy is camping in the souls of the disconsolate. You tell me, John—am I he?"

Have you ever had doubts about me? I cannot answer you any more than I could answer John. When doubts come, do not ask me if I am the Christ. Look around you. You were once self-willed with no hope. You were once living only for your crumbling career. Once your life was out of control, going nowhere. Sin clotted your soul with dark entanglements.

Now you are free.

Now you have hope.

Tell me, am I he?

LORD JESUS,
*I am grateful
that Your life is real enough
to supply all the evidence I need
to trust you most implicitly
for life.*

*I see all that you've in grace achieved
and then cry out in faith, "Lord, I believe."
Amen.*

94

A VOICE FOR THE AGES
IN A DESERT PLACE

LUKE 7:24-28

And when the messengers of John had left, He began to speak to the multitudes about John, "What did you go out into the wilderness to look at? A reed shaken by the wind? But what did you go out to see? A man dressed in soft clothing? Behold, those who are splendidly clothed and live in luxury are found in royal palaces. But what did you go out to see? A prophet? Yes, I say to you, and one who is more than a prophet. This is the one about whom it is written, 'Behold, I send My messenger before your face, Who will prepare Your way before You.' I say to you, among those born of women, there is no one greater than John; yet he who is least in the kingdom of God is greater than he."

LORD,
the person who is but a messenger is one who knows the reason for life. John the Baptizer understood the reason for his life could be summed up in what he was born to tell the world. Why was I born? Tell me what it is I'm to do, that when I am done, it will add up to my life definition.

None are happier than those who know why they are in the world.

John was a rustic trumpet at the end of a grand oratorio. Prophets long before John had announced my coming. This symphony of the prophets resounded with the plaintive poetry of Jeremiah and the high literature of Isaiah. Elijah himself wrote no literature, yet my Father chose Elijah's rural demeanor in the form of John the Baptist to walk once again through the wilderness of Jordan. John was an evidence that my kingdom would be born among the rustic, country folk.

In his own estimation, John was the least of all these prophets. What the other prophets had seen only in the distance, John announced at hand.

I praised John as the greatest of all who were ever naturally born, but with this reservation: It could be that you were born to be even greater. The key to your own exaltation lies in your "leastness." Do you want to know the furthest reaches of my love and own a pedestal in heaven above all the prophets? Then find a wilderness where you may know and love God. In such a desert place, desire to be nothing that you may be all.

Desire oneness with my Father. Out of this craving will come your self-definition—your assignment. You cannot find your calling while you seek some personal platform of recognition. There are two kinds of gifts you should want to give God. The second and most inferior of these gifts are those you take from your material blessings and offer back to him. The first and much preferred offering is the gift of your yieldedness.

This was John's primary gift, his yieldedness. His fiery sermons, his royal rebukes to Herodias, his self-deprecating dress or diet—these courageous gifts grew out of his need for God. From these gifts came a greatness he never saw. Be blind to your own excellence, and your usefulness will be too abundant to be measured.

LORD JESUS,
make me a lonely trumpet
to sound out unmistakably my yieldedness.
Life exists to tell the world
you are God's only Son
and, best of all,
my glorious Lord.

Rejoice, all you who hurt, the Savior comes!
Look, all you blind, and all you feeble, run!
Amen.

95

CHILDREN PLAYING WITH THE JEWELS OF GOD

MATTHEW 11:16-19

But to what shall I compare this generation? It is like children sitting in the market places, who call out to the other children, and say, "We played the flute for you, and you did not dance; we sang a dirge, and you did not mourn." For John came neither eating nor drinking, and they say, "He has a demon!" The Son of Man came eating and drinking, and they say, "Behold, a gluttonous man and a drunkard, a friend of tax-gatherers and sinners!" Yet wisdom is vindicated by her deeds.

LORD, city life seems all concrete and steel. It is not at all the open magic setting where one would expect to find faith. You yourself seemed to notice that where the wild-flowers bloom and the birds sing was a better place for contemplation and faith.

Cities sometimes seem to be hard places to find God. Yet he is there in abundance. For wherever there are many people, God dwells in his fullness. Children forced to play in sandlots and parents trapped in tall steel structures touch the heart of my Father, and he comes in waves of grace to endow their living with meaning.

John lived a solitary life of committed prayer. He lived alone in the jungles of the Jordan. He never drank wine or ate rich foods. He was committed to the simple life. The Pharisees criticized his holy and separated life.

I on the other hand lived in towns and cities. I lived in the middle of crowds of people so that I could reach to save them. Both John and I were criticized. Because I loved immoral partygoers, I too was called a sinner.

How did I view these critics of reality? They were like children who were playing marriage and funeral. Real weddings and real funerals are times of utter commitment and finality. But children in every generation sometimes dress up in their parents clothing to make a pretense of marriage or death.

While I walked on earth, the Pharisees looked past my incarnation and judged me by the mere rules of human convention. I endured it all. I had to become a man. It is impossible to save the blind unless you understand the night. Nor could I redeem the immature without walking in the midst of children.

The Pharisees thought themselves scholars but would not love beyond the rigidity of their stingy doctrines. While they played their churchy games, I came among them, died, and rose again. And yet they were so preoccupied with their consuming petty theologies that they never saw me.

Are you open to those great truths that shatter your comfort level? Love what is holy. Never play petty games when human redemption is at stake. City or country is not the issue of where to look for God. The place of his dwelling is in the starving heart. There he will be found—or nowhere.

LORD JESUS,
how wondrously free is your great salvation.
I cost you everything,
yet you came to me completely packaged,
robed in costly grace
but altogether free.

I want to praise the bearer of such grace,
not play like children in the marketplace.
Amen.

A TALE OF THREE CITIES

MATTHEW 11:20-23

Then He began to reproach the cities in which most of His miracles were done, because they did not repent. "Woe to you, Chorazin! Woe to you, Bethsaida! For if the miracles had occurred in Tyre and Sidon which occurred in you, they would have repented long ago in sackcloth and ashes. Nevertheless I say to you, it shall be more tolerable for Tyre and Sidon in the day of judgment, than for you. And you, Capernaum, will not be exalted to heaven, will you? You shall descend to Hades; for if the miracles had occurred in Sodom which occurred in you, it would have remained to this day.

LORD,
apathy is a harsh reply to the goodness of God. How is it that I, who have been given so much, sometimes forget to care about those who were given little?

The sin of apathy is hidden in this tale of three cities: Chorazin, Bethsaida, and Capernaum. These infamous towns saw the love of God but grew hard toward those who were needy in her streets.

Once upon a time a little girl fell into a well. In the ensuing days before she was rescued, a whole nation came together in prayer. Then at her salvation, the sparkle of her beautiful eyes brought weeping to her grateful world. The world had seen a hurting child rescued, and it was changed.

I have walked through many cities and tried in vain to touch their deadness with life. Yet many of these cities have remained unchanged. Cities are unfeeling centers of humanity where people are murdered on the streets and their cries for help or pity go unheard.

Woe to you, Chorazin, Bethsaida, Capernaum.

Woe to you, all you modern cities filled with unfeeling people.

In a small house a compassionate woman once rescued a sick young gutter sleeper and took her into her home to nurse her back to health. The nurse often kissed this gutter leper as though the power of her affection alone might heal. As she ministered with such kisses, she would often say to herself, *Who knows how much healing there is in a kiss of pity? Who knows but by such a kiss I may bring both salvation and new usefulness to such a one?* On one occasion as she kissed this fevered and dying woman, she came to awareness. She spoke from her delirium, "Thank you," she wept. "Nobody's done that since my mother died." Our kisses may indeed be the only hope the comatose have.

Ministry to those who need God is the only evidence the needy may have that there actually is a God. Yet the busy and self-important come and go unchanged.

Woe to you, Chorazin, Bethsaida, Capernaum!

Woe to all other cities that are like Chorazin, Bethsaida, and Capernaum but named something else! It is a sin to know I am in your streets, saving and healing, and yet not care.

LORD JESUS,
*help me look upon
the world of beauty that's fashioned
in your holy fingers
and promise you,
beneath such canopies of nature,
I'll never doubt you.
Help me see what
beautiful souls you fashion from
ugly but repentant lives.*

*And seeing all you have made evident,
weep and bid my sinful soul repent.
Amen.*

97

CARRY LESS, FEEL BETTER

MATTHEW 11:28-30
Come to Me, all who are weary and heavy-laden, and I will give you rest. Take My yoke upon you, and learn from Me, for I am gentle and humble in heart; and you shall find rest for your souls. For My yoke is easy, and My load is light.

LORD,
I'm tired today. Soul tired. Bone weary. I'm tired deep down. Sometimes living is a heavy weight to be borne. I have borne it. I can go no further.

Are you weary? Are you worn with a draining fatigue of soul that never seems to feel relief? Are you sick and tired of being sick and tired? Come to me; I am the Sabbath Christ. I want to infuse you with Isaiah's words: "They that wait upon the Lord shall renew their strength; they shall mount up with wings as eagles. They shall run and not be weary. They shall walk and not faint" (Isaiah 40:31).

I have told you where to find rest. Now let me tell you why you are tired. You are tired because you stand beneath your yoke alone. You push against the heavy chafing wood all by yourself. You claim I am your Lord, but you are too much lord of your own burdensome affairs.

A certain bedouin once thought to save his camel by carrying himself the burden he would have put on his beast. Are you like that heavily ladened man? Are you struggling to carry the heavy bundles of your own grief to save the back of God? Oh, how foolishly you seek to spare God such labor. Lay aside the heavy gatherings of your own agendas. Put down your staggering determination to be self-made. God longs to give you a lightness of being.

Cast all your cares on me, for I care for you (1 Peter 5:7). Don't struggle with your yoke alone. Above all, lay aside the heavy burden of getting ahead. It is too much for you, and it is so pointless. Stop bragging that you are a self-made person. This boast alone adds to your struggle. My yoke is easy, my burden light.

Come to me and feel the strain of your struggles flow away. Dissolve your fatigue in my sufficiency. Say like the refreshed apostle, "I can do all things through Him who strengthens me" (Philippians 4:13). Then will you sing with new strength, "My God [has supplied] all [my] needs according to His riches in glory in Christ Jesus" (Philippians 4:19). The yoke is light.

LORD JESUS,
so often I am soul fatigued
and bear a lonely, heavy yoke.
How needy. How lonely.
How much I long for your renewing strength.

When trial and turmoil weigh me down with stress,
help me to fly to you, accept your rest.
Amen.

98

GRATITUDE IN TEARS

LUKE 7:36-43

Now one of the Pharisees was requesting Him to dine with him.
And He entered the Pharisee's house, and reclined at the table. And
behold, there was a woman in the city who was a sinner; and when
she learned that He was reclining at the table in the Pharisee's
house, she brought an alabaster vial of perfume, and standing
behind Him at His feet, weeping, she began to wet His feet with
her tears, and kept wiping them with the hair of her head, and
kissing His feet, and anointing them with the perfume. Now when
the Pharisee who had invited Him saw this, he said to himself, "If
this man were a prophet He would know who and what sort of
person this woman is who is touching Him, that she is a sinner."
And Jesus answered and said to him, "Simon, I have something to
say to you." And he replied, "Say it, Teacher." "A certain money-
lender had two debtors: one owed five hundred denarii, and the
other fifty. When they were unable to repay, he graciously forgave
them both. Which of them therefore will love him more?" Simon
answered and said, "I suppose the one whom he forgave more."
And He said to him, "You have judged correctly."

LORD, sometimes I feel that religious people are so concerned
about how they look to each other, they never let down
their guard long enough to be real. If we cannot show
how we feel, we will soon not feel a thing. Can you help
me be real? A public tear, shed in honesty, is better than
the cold and formal need to suppress it just so I'll appear
in control to my perfectly proper friends.

When you understand both your unworthiness and God's great grace,
you will weep. Not all the cold propriety in the world will stop a single hot
and honest tear. You cannot help but prostrate yourself before your bene-
factor and let your tears be witness to your gratitude.

Consider this woman. Her moral reputation was poor. She had crashed a party given by those who considered themselves far above her social caste. Yet she dared to come in among the elite and wash my feet with her tears.

Of course she wasn't doing the proper thing. Her emotions were out of control.

But then propriety and true joy are rarely found in the same place at the same time. Nor are high liturgy and utter brokenness. But God inhabits the real far more often than the rehearsed. So the sinful woman came, overwhelmed by a loving God who had forgiven her. Her alleluias were unstoppable.

Those who were there saw her as contemptuous. But blessed are the needy, for they are so overwhelmed by the goodness of God that they must shout their alleluias openly. One thing is sure: To feel sinfulness washed with forgiveness leaves no one silent. You are no different from her. Touched with such a lightness of being, you too must wake the town and tell the people. You must crash the party and praise him who is the great Forgiver.

I am not devious, but I most enjoyed the woman's unwelcome presence among the Pharisees. They were all set to talk theology with me when she broke into the room. She *did* theology. *Talking it* was not enough for her. I am sure, had she not come, we would have talked about the theological ins and outs of intellectual forgiveness and thankfulness. The Pharisees would have used the right footnotes and quoted the right sources.

But triumph held the day! Real forgiveness had danced its way into their academics.

How is it with you? Are you more interested in religious discussions than you are in praise? Would you rather teach a lesson on forgiveness than have it ravage you with open joy?

LORD JESUS,
I want to be
more exhibitionist in my
love for you.
I do not want to be sharing for
the sake of showiness
but to let everyone know
how glorious it is to be forgiven.

I must declare your grace with gratitude
and openly make joy my attitude.
Amen.

99

THE WOMEN OF GOD

And also some women who had been healed of evil spirits and sicknesses: Mary who was called Magdalene, from whom seven demons had gone out, and Joanna the wife of Chuza, Herod's steward, and Susanna, and many others who were contributing to their support out of their private means.

LORD,
I can't help noticing that women hold too little place in the service of God. Men so often run the show, while women, sitting farther back in the church, sit quietly and let the kingdom of God appear to be the providence of the men. Is this right? Do women have a place? Should they rise to take it?

Women have often found the church too closed. Every day of my life, women were the most consistent of my supporters. What shall I say of Luke's glorious Gospel? This wonderful biographer of mine begs us shout the triumph of those women who supported me.

Let me not injure the insurgency of angry feminism in this day. Often women have a right to be angry, for they have often been pushed aside and held down in a world long dominated by men. But for the moment let's not talk—men or women—of seizing all we have a right to seize. Instead, let us talk about our voluntary laying aside of those things that we have every right to own.

More than all the other Gospel writers, Luke seemed to sense the importance of women to my life and ministry. Why were these women so important? Because they were willing to lay down their lives for my sake. They did not argue their right to run the kingdom of God. They simply demonstrated the submission that ought to belong to either gender.

Consider my mother, Mary. While my own mother is not mentioned in Luke 8, so much of Luke's Gospel is clearly privy to information only my mother could have known: the birth stories, the reaction of the Nazarenes.

So in a way it is not unthinkable to see Luke's Gospel as Mary's Gospel—at least in part.

So then let us not speak of the great men of God without speaking of the great women of God. It is even as Paul says in Galatians 3:28-29 (NIV), "There is neither Jew nor Greek, slave nor free, male nor female, for you are all one in Christ Jesus. If you belong to Christ, then you are Abraham's seed, and heirs according to the promise."

Disciples come in both genders!

So do martyrs.

Those who really love me offer only their commitment as credentials. Never is their gender too significant.

LORD JESUS,

I know so many women
who follow you in utter adoration.
They have surrendered all,
yet often they have struggled
with their self-esteem.
Father, forgive us when we fail
to honor those whose gender
has sometimes relegated them to second class.
Help me to see that you do not see men and women
as separate kinds of people to be loved in separate ways.
That's how I want to see people—
just like you do.

The church must gather for your adoration
and cast before your cross, discrimination.
Amen.

100

DISTINGUISHING GOOD AND EVIL

MATTHEW 12:22-26
Then there was brought to Him a demon-possessed man who was blind and dumb, and He healed him, so that the dumb man spoke and saw. And all the multitudes were amazed, and began to say, "This man cannot be the Son of David, can he?" But when the Pharisees heard it, they said, "This man casts out demons only by Beelzebul the ruler of the demons." And knowing their thoughts He said to them, "Any kingdom divided against itself is laid waste; and any city or house divided against itself shall not stand. And if Satan casts out Satan, he is divided against himself; how then shall his kingdom stand?"

LORD,
are there really demons and devils? Or are they just a loophole in our refusal to give up our childhood fears? They seem so akin to ghouls and hobgoblins and things that go bump in the night. Are they just supernatural definitions of bad luck?

I consider the casting out of demons to be the most significant of all my miracles. Consider the great amount of space that is given to exorcisms in the four Gospels. Why? Because demons represent the unlawful incursion of Satan into the sanctity of the human soul. Every human life is sacred. Everyone is made by my Father to celebrate his holiness. What right does the Enemy think he has to invade those lives so loved by God?

I lived my entire life being tempted in all points like every other person, and yet I never sinned (Hebrews 4:15). During my lifetime, however, I received this most bizarre of criticisms. Some said it was only because I was filled with Satan that he enabled me to cast demons out of others.

It is a confused state of thinking that cannot distinguish good and evil. If a thing is evil, it is not from God. If it is good, it can be from nowhere else. But as simple as this rule is, good men and women sometimes believe that they can do some temporary evil that will, in the end, bring about everlasting good. Do not believe it. No good grain ever sprung from evil soil.

The Crusades were the monumental failures of those Christians who believed they could make war to establish peace. Pious Christian warriors felt that if they waged death with great effectiveness, they could bring forth life. They tortured unbelievers to the point of madness to get them to confess Christianity. Being flayed alive, many cried out that they did believe in me. The horror of these forced confessions still mark the earth with old undying hatreds.

Satan's greatest lie is that he can help us, through acts of evil, to arrive finally at good. Never adopt such logic. Good fruit cannot come from a corrupt tree.

Only righteousness can come from God. The Pharisees were wrong. I could never be so filled with Satan that I would do God's will. I had only one answer for the Enemy. "I have come to do Your will, O God" (Hebrews 10:9 NKJV).

Stand up to your temptations in the power of God. When you have finished, angels will come and minister unto you (Matthew 4:11). You may not see them, but they will be there.

LORD JESUS,
I want to avoid
the idea that I can trade
some little lies
to buy some greater truths.
Help me to be
a person who never attempts
to arrive at constant values
with flexible righteousness.

Evil always camps out in the soul
when godly faith abandons self-control.
Amen.

101

THE UNFORGIVABLE SIN

MATTHEW 12:30-32

He who is not with Me is against Me; and he who does not gather with Me scatters. Therefore I say to you, any sin and blasphemy shall be forgiven men, but blasphemy against the Spirit shall not be forgiven. And whoever shall speak a word against the Son of Man, it shall be forgiven him; but whoever shall speak against the Holy Spirit, it shall not be forgiven him, either in this age, or in the age to come.

LORD,
I fear the word *unforgivable*. Why? I suppose it seems a chink in God's ability to forgive all sin. Is there one step of caprice I dare not take? Is there some sin so unforgivable that God will say I went too far? Have I the ability to do something so wrong, God will at last say to me, "With this you went too far. Be damned forever!"?

Yes, there is one such sin. It is to shout in the face of pure love, "I despise you!" But you are surely wondering, *What has the Holy Spirit to do with this unforgivable sin?* The Holy Spirit is the indwelling God. He woos the hearts of human beings in the name of the Almighty's love. He knocks in my name to seek entrance to your heart. He desires to live in you. To refuse to let him in is the sin of inhospitality to God.

Walk outside on any starry night. Look up into the face of a thousand unnamed galaxies and solar systems. Realize that he who made all this made you as well. He made you for himself. Tell me now, what right have you to refuse such a grand God an entrance to your lowly heart? What right have you to say no to your Father? Indeed, I stand at the door and knock; if anyone hears and opens I will come in. Yet many customarily refuse me. Nations refuse me, churches refuse me, and individuals refuse me.

Would you refuse me too?

To leave me standing outside while the Spirit begs entrance is a dangerous refusal. It is this inhospitality of heart that is the unforgivable sin. It begins in the simple refusal to let me in.

Hell rarely begins in grand and blatant blasphemy but rather in weak intent. It is not belligerent atheists who fill the halls of hell. It is the good men or women who wanted to know God but believed that knowing him sometime later would be soon enough. It is this someday saint who arrives in eternity still saying, "Not today, God...Not today, God...Not today, God."

Can you not see this? Blasphemy against the Holy Ghost is not usually some grand and single moment of cursing God. No, it is rather a thousand micro-denials of "Not now, please." These tiny Lilliputian threads at last stake you down just outside the gates of heaven.

Are you guilty of saying no to God? Are you forever slapping the gentle fingers of your reaching Father? He will not enter your heart without your open invitation. Hell has but a small population of grand blasphemers. It is filled mostly with warm procrastinators who never saw their weak intentions as dangerous.

LORD JESUS,
The road to eternal separation
rarely begins when we order
You from our lives.
The final barring
of our souls from heaven
comes as we ignore the gentle
rapping of the gentle hand of love.

The only sin beyond the Savior's face
is that which will not yield to love and grace.
Amen.

102

THE JONAH SIGN

MATTHEW 12:38-40

Then some of the scribes and Pharisees answered Him, saying, "Teacher, we want to see a sign from You." But He answered and said to them, "An evil and adulterous generation craves for a sign; and yet no sign shall be given to it but the sign of Jonah the prophet; for just as Jonah was three days and three nights in the belly of the sea monster, so shall the Son of Man be three days and three nights in the heart of the earth."

LORD, I need help believing. If only I could see one little miracle, it would be easier to cling to faith. You don't have to split a sea to make me happy; just dry up a mud puddle or change a little of my water into wine. Could you help me? It is so hard coming to faith without a little support.

"Give us a sign," said the Pharisees. "Please, pull some divine rabbit—even a little one—out of your celestial hat, and we will believe."

I wanted to say to them, "Yes, magic will convince you, but for how long? Till you doubt another time and need another trick? There will never be enough rabbits in my hat to keep you from forever running back in future moments of doubt."

"Here is my only sign." I said to them, "As Jonah was in the belly of the sea monster for three days and nights, even so shall the Son of Man be in the heart of the earth."

My words were cryptic to them then. Only later, after that first tomb-splitting Easter would they understand. In the meantime I refused to give them what they wanted so I could give them what they needed. What they needed was not a sign. Signs are like fireworks exploding against a dark sky. You love them. They bring the oohs and aahs from spectators. Sadly, however, you are lost to recall their precise form once the sky is black again. You strain to try and feel again what cannot be refelt.

So instead of signs, I have given you one great truth. I am that truth. Those who trust in me and in all I am will be saved. My presence may at times seem less immediate than you would like. When you are torn with grief, I may seem out of reach. Surely you have had such moments when you cried out to me and I seemed absent, haven't you?

Of course you have. I ache for you at such times. But do not despair. For in these reaching, racking moments of your awful aloneness, your need will always bring me close. And my closeness will reward you, not because you saw a miracle but because you trusted what cannot be seen.

Faith alone saves, not signs. Therefore, when you pray and cannot feel my nearness, keep on trusting. I will come. Until that time, I give you only that same sign I gave the sign-mongers of the first century—the sign of Jonah. I was dead in the cold earth and came forth in triumph. Behold, I am alive forevermore. Such a sign is all you need. An eternal promise from an eternal Savior is always better than a temporary trick.

LORD JESUS,
require of me more faith.
I want to see
those things
that require the deliciousness
of trust.

But I am so frustrated by my doubts;
excise my fears and drive the demons out.
Amen.

103

LESSONS ON FILLING
THE EMPTY HEART

MATTHEW 12:43-45

Now when the unclean spirit goes out of a man, it passes through waterless places, seeking rest, and does not find it. Then it says, "I will return to my house from which I came"; and when it comes, it finds it unoccupied, swept, and put in order. Then it goes, and takes along with it seven other spirits more wicked than itself, and they go in and live there; and the last state of that man becomes worse than the first. That is the way it will also be with this evil generation.

LORD,
I feel empty today. My soul is clean. There is an echo in my vacuous heart. I contain nothing. I feel nothing. Is this kind of emptiness dangerous to faith?

It is dangerous. Vacuums are desperate empty places. Why? There is something that doesn't like a vacuum. To exorcise a host of heavy demons brings a marvelous buoyancy. The heart that was full of anguish is suddenly clean and empty. But beware the exhilaration that comes from this new cleanness. Emptiness is never the point of God's cleansing. He empties us of evil only to fill us with himself. It is a mistake to celebrate too fast or too long that good clean feeling you had when first you came to know me.

See your longing soul as a bucket that can be lowered on a long rope in order to bring up clear, cold water from a well. Neither the bucket nor your soul can be filled beyond the capacity of your emptiness. If the pail is full of rocks when you lower it into the deep water, when you draw it out you will bring up both water and rocks. If you would have the rising bucket completely full of water when you bring it up, it must be completely empty when you send it down.

God cleansed you so that your emptiness may become a vessel for his use. He wants to refresh the world through your life. God never wants you to celebrate your emptiness but rather your coming fullness. Only if your cleansing comes with a yearning to be filled can you ever serve him.

Do you see that exorcisms may heal you either terminally or temporally? The choice is yours. If the demons that leave your life are not replaced by his fullness, they will be back. Have you not known some outstanding convert, some secular hero, who came to me, purged of a squalid lifestyle? For a while, such cleansed souls acquire more adulation than they received when they were secular heroes. But soon Christian ego takes the place of the celebrity ego, for no real filling of God has taken place. Soon the original devil is back with seven of his friends. Not only is faith abandoned but the glory of the testimony is lost.

Come to me and be clean. Do not leave the altar too soon. Send down the bucket of your need into my cold, deep, pure supply. Let the rope lengthen and the vessel descend into the cold, clean influx. Then your empty soul will fill with godly substance, and the world that reaches out for my Father will find him squarely in the middle of your clean, full life.

LORD JESUS,
create in me a clean heart, O God,
and renew a right spirit within me.
Cast me not away from your presence,
and take not your Holy Spirit from me.

Purge me with hyssop, and clean shall I go.
Wash me, and I shall be whiter than snow.
Amen.

104

WHO IS YOUR FAMILY?

MATTHEW 12:46-50
While He was still speaking to the multitudes, behold, His mother
and brothers were standing outside, seeking to speak to Him. And
someone said to Him, "Behold, Your mother and Your brothers
are standing outside seeking to speak to You." But He answered
the one who was telling Him and said, "Who is My mother and
who are My brothers?" And stretching out His hand toward His
disciples, He said, "Behold, My mother and My brothers! For
whoever does the will of My Father who is in heaven, he is My
brother and sister and mother."

LORD,
I need a family that's always there. Sometimes my family
is too critical of me. They are of my blood but not nearly
so nice to me as these friends I prefer to be around. It is
well said, "You get to choose your friends but not your
family." How can I learn to see them in a better light?

Families are not easy to live with even though you're born into them.
But families do have one great virtue: They feel together the sting of public
scandal.

My family knew from the first my own unique roll in human redemption. They felt a strong sense of rebuke when so much negative community
conversation broke all around me. Mary knew more than them all, for she
was there that long-ago night the Eastern kings came to adore me. She too
heard old Simeon say that a sword would pierce her own soul through. My
family knew that having a Messiah in the family would not be easy. Still,
when the storm of criticism gathered around my ministry, they came to
take me home. The phrase *take me home* really meant "shut me up."

Good Friday was especially hard on them. No one likes to have a
convicted felon in the family. I understand how they must have felt, and
yet I yearned for their affirmation in my time of popular rejection. If the

family understands, one can bear all that must be borne. Given a good home life, a person can endure anything.

During every lifetime, some crisis comes to each home that evokes the utmost in understanding. I was a grown man when my mother sought me out. And yet, in regard to the home and family, in some ways we are always needy children.

I experienced much rejection in my life, but none of it hurt more than the knowledge that my family refused to have confidence in me. Judgments within the family are the most damaging to your development. When families reject you, there is but one alternate course: You must widen your families to those who will accept you and those who will affirm you. It was not to hurt my mother or any of my siblings that I turned to the crowd to ask, "Who are my brothers, my sisters, my mother? Who is my family? Those who understand and do the will of God. It is those who reached to me in confidence and faith."

Where do you go to church? Do you prize that church? Let it be your family at those moments when you are emotionally needy. Is there someone in your church who needs a sister to embrace her? Who is there among your Christian brothers who has not lost a job or a child along life's way? Be to such needy ones a brother or a sister. Be a mother to the orphans. Be a quiet friend to grieving widows. The needy believers in your world are your family.

Serve them.

Heal them.

Love them!

LORD JESUS,
it is hard to be a Christian
among those who really know us.
But help me see my own family
as a wonderful gathering
of all the most supportive folks I know.
May all of us within our homes

see all your children as our family
and know you love them just as you love me.
Amen.

105

THE MYSTERY IS THE TRUSTEE OF TRUTH

MATTHEW 13:10-11,13

And the disciples came and said to Him, "Why do You speak to them in parables?" And He answered and said to them, "To you it has been granted to know the mysteries of the kingdom of heaven, but to them it has not been granted...Therefore I speak to them in parables; because while seeing they do not see, and while hearing they do not hear, nor do they understand."

LORD,
the kingdom seems plain—and may I say, boring. Why? Why don't preachers seem more interesting? I sometimes envy ushers who get to stay out in the hall while the money is counted. I want to learn more about you, but I hate being bored while I do. What makes preachers so boring?

There is no single answer to this, but if there were it would likely lie in the realm of story. If more preachers worked on their storytelling, church would not seem so much like a long, hot ride through a dry gulch. So often my kingdom stories seemed to befuddle those who wanted pat-answer truths in printed codes and precepts. But at least I never bored people. Parables hold a double power. They put into flesh and bone those commandments some would not hear if they were not in story form. But best of all, stories rivet our attention, while plodding precepts only plunge us into boredom.

If you would teach and hold interest, tell stories. Wrap your greatest truths in "once upon a times," and all will hear you gladly. There is no truth too heavy to bear if you can put it in a story.

Why did I deliberately cloak the message of the kingdom in these elusive stories? The reason is clear: The same parables clearly understood by my friends befuddled my enemies with confusion. Had not the prophet Isaiah written, "You will keep on hearing but will not understand; and you will keep on seeing but will not perceive; for the heart of this people has become dull, and with their ears they scarcely hear, and they have closed their eyes lest they should see with their eyes" (Matthew 13:14-15)?

Those dull of hearing had blunted their knowledge of God with a thousand secondary laws. So I told them stories. Thus they heard my tales dance brisk truth into their open hearts.

My stories held the magic of mystery. After my ascension, the story impulse continued. The stories of my life and resurrection were called Gospels. The stories within the Gospel were called parables. The stories of the young church were called the Acts of the Apostles. And, best of all, the story of your own affair with me is called your personal testimony. My church has ever gathered around the Apostle's Creed, which is a story confession, recounting how I was born, lived, died, rose, and am coming again.

Story is the teaching method of the kingdom of God. Eyes grown blind from studying narrow precepts will miss much. The sing-song repetition of legal codes will never hold the unfolding of the mystery of those kingdom stories that the church still gathers to celebrate.

The story redeems. The story praises. The story instructs. The great "once upon a times" of the Gospels are but God's carriages of truth, in which the needy, at last, arrive spell-bound into the kingdom.

LORD JESUS,
your parables
were narrative wrappers
in which you packaged
your eternal truth.

I want to make your kingdom stories grand
as sleeves of love that hide your wounded hands.
Amen.

106

THE ROADSIDE SOIL

MATTHEW 13:18-19
Hear then the parable of the sower. When anyone hears the word
of the kingdom, and does not understand it, the evil one comes
and snatches away what has been sown in his heart. This is the one
on whom seed was sown beside the road.

L ORD,
my faith, as I've confessed to you, is at times quite
small—very small. I would wish it were stronger and
more robust. How can I enlarge something so small into
something sufficiently large?

Never despise faith for being small; nearly all faith begins that way. But
it will grow. In my story, the birds came and devoured the seed that fell
beside the road. This devoured seed was a picture of Satan's determination
to stop all growth in the kingdom. But do not give the devouring birds your
focus. The central symbol of this parable is the seed. Each small seed
contained a very small plant, eager to reproduce itself. Warmed by sunlight,
such tiny seedlings are driven sunward by a single dream: They must mature
to keep their kind alive upon the earth. The power of their zeal to reproduce can only be called plant power.

Consider this plant power for a moment.

A seed, though tiny, has only to drink the smallest sip of water to be
moved by a kind of drivenness. It will reach upward for sunlight even
though it has been planted underneath solid stone. It will burst through
tarmac and split pavement. It will, with small but certain force, dislodge
foundation stones. The unrelenting life force of the small seed is determined
by its need to reach the sun.

Here lies the parable within the parable. The seed must see itself as a
full-grown plant bearing seeds of its own. Can any seed lament its size?
Does a seed inside a redwood cone lie on the ground beneath the tree that
spawned it and despair? Does it look at its giant redwood parent and
lament, "I could never be that!"? No, it handles the issue of its own

becoming by taking one step at a time: a little earth, a little water, a little time. Never letting the size of its destiny challenge the immediate moment, it puts first things first. It splits its jacket and sends out only a tiny thread of life that longs for *treedom*. Then presto! One hundred years! A tree! Then somewhere from its own towering branches, it drops a cone whose eager seeds beget again the same patient yearning to be trees themselves.

But what of these seeds in my story? What of this specific seed dropped by the wayside? Poor seed. No destiny for this small seed. It is eaten quickly by the birds of the air. No growth. No maturity. No destiny. Satan can stop the kingdom growth in any life. He sometimes does devour the destiny of those who will not find a life within the nourishing of better soil.

LORD JESUS,
I treasure that small faith
I hold within my heart.
May I give it time.
May I nourish it and trust.
May I feed my faith and let it grow.

I'll trust that faith I hold in embryo
and thrill to watch this seedling grow.
Amen.

107

ROOTLESSNESS

Matthew 13:20-21

And the one on whom seed was sown on the rocky places, this is the man who hears the word, and immediately receives it with joy; yet he has no firm root in himself, but is only temporary, and when affliction or persecution arises because of the word, immediately he falls away.

LORD,
I seem today to feel so wishy-washy. I'm drifting in my devotion to you. How can I attach myself to a growing, thriving faith?

Remember, no plant can thrive without a root. Cut the root, and the plant will die. In my parable of the soils, some seed falls into ground that is hard—there the soil allows only for a shallow root. There is barely enough earth to warm the seed and hardly enough moisture to entice it to grow. The plant springs up quickly. But there is not enough earth to give it root. When the sun rises, the new sprout of promise is scorched and lost.

You are wise to be concerned about rootlessness. Rootlessness is the curse of the church. Too many churches keep up an appearance of good nourishment but have roots that are shallow. Amos the prophet wrote of that spiritual shallowness that would characterize the kingdom at the end of time:

> "The days are coming," declares the Sovereign LORD, "when I will send a famine through the land—not a famine of food or a thirst for water, but a famine of hearing the words of the LORD. Men will stagger from sea to sea and wander from north to east, searching for the word of the LORD, but they will not find it. In that day the lovely young women and strong young men will faint because of thirst. They who swear by the shame of Samaria, or say, 'As surely as your god lives,

O Dan,' or, 'As surely as the god of Beersheba lives'—
they will fall, never to rise again" (Amos 8:11-14).

The hunger in your heart for the knowledge of God is immense. The
root of your nourishment should be the Word of God. You are wise to be
concerned, for there is in every age a famine for the hearing of the words
of the Lord.

Your church has the obligation to nourish you with the Scriptures. You
know you are hungry. You do not always know what to do with your
hungers. The prophet describes your searching: Those who are rootless fly
from church to church, from new idea to new idea. They try out each new
"ism" and read hungrily through every new manual of discipleship. They
never stay with any new idea long enough to put down roots, and soon
their frantic search ends in spiritual anemia and death.

Seek me on your own within the Word. But seek me beyond the hassled,
hurried searching that ends in spiritual death. Plant yourself—develop a
little root. Wait and grow. And this I promise: You will grow. Just stay
attached.

LORD JESUS,
the life of Christ
is needed in the shallow
secular soul I sometimes feel
I have become.
Help me to nourish myself
by being sure I am rooted
in the fertile soil of your
plan for my life.
I realize that

if I am too weakly nourished in the root,
my faith will suffer, trodden underfoot.
Amen.

108

DEATH BY STRANGULATION

MATTHEW 13:22

And the one on whom seed was sown among the thorns, this is the man who hears the word, and the worry of the world, and the deceitfulness of riches choke the word, and it becomes unfruitful.

LORD,
my job isn't going well. I have family problems. My life is on hold, and I cannot seem to get ahead. Besides all this, the first of the month is coming, and the bills will bury me in hopelessness. Why? I can't pay them. I go to bed with a headache and get up with a bad taste in my mouth. As you can tell—my complaint list seems to be growing. I am not the picture of victory. I'm beat!

When the vitality of your life is choked by worldly cares, it is usually the result of your choices. Your problem is serious but of your own making. The thorns of your circumstances can choke you nearly to death, but only when you give them permission to do it.

Consider two people who embrace Christianity at the same time. One of them goes on to live a powerful life while the other winds up a defeated dropout. Is it because one of them has a more difficult set of circumstances than the other? Generally not. Each of their destinies is a matter of their individual choices. At every juncture of our lives we choose our futures, and therefore we choose our moods. No one ever forces us to laugh or weep; we consciously choose mirth or gloom.

Are you sweltering under despair? Blame it not on your circumstances. Happiness is an option, but so is despair. If you are dominated by darkness, you have given gloom the right to camp in your soul by saying yes to the darkness. You can as easily order gloom from your soul by saying no to the darkness. Thorns do strangle, but only with your permission.

Job had his moments of despair. Still, he did not always allow his moods to own the day. When he had every right to say no, he said yes and cried, "Though he slay me, yet will I trust in him" (Job 13:15 KJV).

Let your tangled circumstances become your counselors. Then confess, "Lord, I know this pain has come from you. Teach me your triumph. Teach me that crosses are often the result of overwhelming and crushing circumstances. But even on your cross, Jesus, you did not complain of life's unfairness. Nor did you let despair steal from you the certain knowledge of your destiny. Lord, help me when my vision blurs with weeping. Never let my own cross make me bitter."

LORD JESUS,
stress makes me feel
I've drifted beyond your help
and keeps me looking too low
for a way out of my troubles.
Help me to see that

when I make misery my pouting meal,
I'm still the captain of the way I feel.
Amen.

109

THE GOOD EARTH

MATTHEW 13:23
And the one on whom seed was sown on the good soil, this is the
man who hears the word and understands it; who indeed bears
fruit, and brings forth, some a hundred fold, some sixty, and some
thirty.

LORD, there's nothing like feeling productive. I'm back on top.
I'm in charge. I feel useful and productive.

It is a good feeling to know that good things are flowing from your life.
The good earth in this parable of the soils is that in which the seed takes
root, matures, and produces a thousand grains of wheat. Yet each stalk of
wheat was once just a seed. Did the seed that produced a hundred other
seeds ever struggle to out-succeed the less productive seeds it slept with in
the sower's bag? Did the tiny seed ask how it could become the tallest and
the richest through competition? Of course not. It merely took life one step
at a time while God supplied the sun and water.

If it is not too humorous to imagine…good soil is productive, and
productive soil is happy. This must also be said of good people like you.
There is a yearning in your life to produce something of value. Do you not
want to feel like you are creating something worthy from the substance of
your life? The majority of suicide notes—however self-pitying their
message—ask questions like these: "What good am I? What have I
produced? What have I ever done that gives me any good reasons to go on
living another day?"

Artifacts are those bits of cultural bric-a-brac that describe for us what
the former inhabitants of the earth were like. These bits of pottery or rusted
implements were created out of the human need to make something. With
their making of such artifacts these ancient souls would say, "This is of
me—mine—I made it." Now such ancient artists are gone, and only that
which they made tell us they ever existed.

My Father loves you simply for making his world your address. He loves you unconditionally whether your life ever produces anything or not. But while God loves you for simply existing, he knows you have a need to own the pride of making something useful. For then you will feel yourself truly made in the image of God. Like the world around you, you have a longing to say, "Here's what's issuing from my life." To create is a part of the *imago dei*, the image of God. The universe and all that is in it says God is a Maker. But this is the heart cry of your own soul: "See, I am a maker too! Behold what issues from my life. My life draws meaning from the good things it produces."

The good soil in my parable knows the pride of taking something little and being willing to be the matrix of the creativity of God. Think about the product of one little grain of wheat—one little seed taking off its coat and going to work. This self-replicating seed pushes through its tiny little filament stalk 100,000 times the substance of its flimsy self until it has made a huge plant. Not the brightest person in the world can explain the miracle of harvest, but even the dullest may enjoy bread. You are part of it all. You are like God. You can make your world produce. You are good soil.

LORD JESUS,
I want to feel your power
stirring in my life.
I want to create something beautiful
that I may leave it here
to point others toward eternity and truth.
I too am created imago dei—
in the image of God.

As you but spoke and worlds came to be,
I want to speak forth life and victory.
Amen.

110

WEEDS

MATTHEW 13:24-30

He presented another parable to them, saying, "The kingdom of heaven may be compared to a man who sowed good seed in his field. But while men were sleeping, his enemy came and sowed tares also among the wheat, and went away. But when the wheat sprang up and bore grain, then the tares became evident also. And the slaves of the landowner came and said to him, 'Sir, did you not sow good seed in your field? How then does it have tares?' And he said to them, 'An enemy has done this!' And the slaves said to him, 'Do you want us, then, to go and gather them up?' But he said, 'No; lest while you are gathering up the tares, you may root up the wheat with them. Allow both to grow together until the harvest; and in the time of the harvest I will say to the reapers, "First gather up the tares and bind them in bundles to burn them up; but gather the wheat into my barn."'"

LORD,
you probably know this, but I go to church with a lot of slow learners. Confidentially, I suspect a lot of them aren't true believers like I am. They don't seem as sincere as me. How can I go on living the good life in the middle of a lot of gospel students who are just not A-plus?

Could you be stuck on yourself? If I asked the people who go to your church, would they say the same thing about you?

Unregenerate members are pictured in my parables as weeds.

The final harvest of heaven will include some weeds. Weeds take advantage of the soft earth that was cultivated for the sake of the grain. Weeds sink their roots into soil they never deserved. When the grain is fertilized, the weeds eat up nutrients never intended for them. They devour the sunlight meant to nourish the grain.

They are obnoxious and intrusive. Yet it is not possible to grow much grain without them. The question is how to get rid of them. If you try to crush them beneath your heel, you will also crush the good plants. If you try to pull the weeds up, you will uproot the grain.

The best way to handle weeds is to let them grow till harvest, and then they may be burned up when the grain is harvested.

Fire is the final test of all that is usable or not. In the New Testament, my customary word for hell was *Gehenna. Gehenna* was a word that grew out of an old Hebrew word, *Hinnom.* Hinnom was a valley once used by pagans for fiery child sacrifice. But by New Testament times the valley had become a place where the city trash was burned. By New Testament times it was merely called Gehenna, the trash dump outside Jerusalem. Visitors and citizens coming in and out of this city could never remember entering or leaving Jerusalem without seeing the thin tendrils of smoke rising from this dump. It appeared that in Gehenna the fire never stopped—the smoke was there forever—a fairly adequate picture of hell, a place where the "fire was never quenched and the worm did not die" (Mark 9:48).

But what is the nature of the trash that fuels such fires? Trash is composed of things discarded, for they no longer have value. Weeds fit the description. God in final judgment will burn the refuse to make room for the valuable.

Forget the weeds. Focus on the grain. In the final writing of life, only the grain will commend you to God.

LORD JESUS,
no flawlessness can come to any life,
and so I must live with
all the warts and wrinkles
of my own imperfect life.
Weeds are rank in the untilled acres
of my philosophies.
Yet I know how to deal with weeds.

I give to you the grainfields of my deeds.
Receive the grain, eliminate the weeds.
Amen.

111

THE MUSTARD-SEED KINGDOM

MATTHEW 13:31-32

He presented another parable to them, saying, "The kingdom of heaven is like a mustard seed, which a man took and sowed in his field; and this is smaller than all other seeds; but when it is full grown, it is larger than the garden plants, and becomes a tree, so that the birds of the air come and nest in its branches."

LORD,
why am I still so close to the starting place in my life? I was confirmed in the faith. I've always gone to church. But I still seem like a beginner in all I need to learn and what I want to become. I want to serve you and see my life become significant in all the wonderful things you're trying to do in your world. Why am I still feeling like an adolescent in a grown-up's world?

You are far too hard on yourself. You are more mature than you think you are. But you are right to be concerned about the issue of coming to maturity as a Christian. Growth is good.

Growth is the principle of all that is healthy. If any organism is getting bigger and if it is not diseased, its growth is of God. This mustard seed, like the seeds of grain I mentioned in so many other parables, contains a life principle. This mustard seed, like a grain of wheat, holds within its speck of near invisibility, a very little plant yearning to grow. Once it germinates, it will become a tree so huge that the birds of the world can rest in its branches. Between the microscopic speck of the mustard seed and the adult tree it produces lies the nourishing of God.

My church has grown slowly from a tiny little seed of its beginning. There the warm soil of Calvary and the balmy winds of Pentecost nourished my infant church. Now it stretches its arms around the globe. This is true of individual churches as well. Here in the local church, the mustard seed must be your example. I intended the local church to grow. Not every great church is a big church, but every great church is a growing church.

But remember this: It is possible to make a fetish out of church growth. Is the church not sometimes guilty of using marketing and advertising tactics that seek to make it bigger without making it great? Of course, many do. But wherever my Spirit is given full reign to act in individual ways with individual congregations, it will grow.

What of those churches that cannot grow much because they are in areas where the population is declining? There ministers and people should allow the mustard seed of growth to enlarge their hearts. Members of these growth-locked congregations can learn to serve beyond the borders of their declining communities. In a rural or isolated community where the church cannot get bigger by adding members, the members should at least be getting bigger in their understanding of my mission to the world beyond its walls.

The kingdom must grow. Growth is the destiny of the healthy church. Praise is its energy. Joy marks the journey. So should it be with your life.

LORD JESUS,
help me to see
that a child that will not grow
may be very loved,
but it is not healthy.
Help me to earnestly desire
to mature to ever greater
levels of responsibility
and understanding.

I want to grow to fit my destiny
and serve and hunger for maturity.
Amen.

112

THE YEAST

MATTHEW 13:33-35

He spoke another parable to them, "The kingdom of heaven is like leaven, which a woman took, and hid in three pecks of meal, until it was all leavened." All these things Jesus spoke to the multitudes in parables, and He did not speak to them without a parable, so that what was spoken through the prophet might be fulfilled, saying, "I will open My mouth in parables; I will utter things hidden since the foundation of the world."

LORD, change is the order of the kingdom. I once foolishly thought that I would do all my changing at that wonderful first moment of faith. But now I realize that life in Christ is a matter of constantly changing all through life. Conforming my life to the form of Christ is a lifelong business.

The yeast in this story represents the pervasive movement of change that will go on throughout your life. It is correct to believe that God and heaven are always there. But you may have a tendency to speak of the unchanging nature of God as too fixed. You may soon be prone to see him as always there and always the same. Do not believe it. Those scientists who teach the expanding universe are right. God invades—really he pervades—the entire cosmos. The universe is his home. He is constantly enlarging it as he continually grows to fill it.

Oddly, this process describes all that God touches, even to the least of my disciples. Yes, the yeast of God's all-pervading Spirit now fills your life. If your compassion and your heart of adoration are not growing, you frustrate the yeast of the Spirit. Selfish little Christians sometimes try to keep God and their church in a stingy little box of sameness. To miniaturize God till he slips comfortably inside a zipper Bible is to miss him altogether. When the yeast of the Spirit permeates the dough, the loaf must grow.

All the attributes of God are designed to enlarge within you as God grows within you. So never champion the status quo. A little mind content in a little system, practicing the contented rules of churchmanship, will never be much like God. Growth always happens on the cusp of courage. Be brave therefore. Try new ideas, walk new roads. Let the yeast within you enlarge your soul.

LORD JESUS,
it is your nature
to fill all the universe,
and in your growing presence
I can see
that you must live and grow
inside of me as well.

Grow inside my waiting life like yeast.
Grace is the wine, and love shall be the feast.
Amen.

113

THE TREASURE
AND THE PEARL

MATTHEW 13:44-46
The kingdom of heaven is like a treasure hidden in the field, which
a man found and hid; and from joy over it he goes and sells all
that he has, and buys that field. Again, the kingdom of heaven is
like a merchant seeking fine pearls, and upon finding one pearl of
great value, he went and sold all that he had, and bought it.

LORD,
I have found it! The treasure is mine. I once had no
destiny, but I found it! I once was content with selfish
living, and then I found it! It's mine! I had nothing, and
then I was rich. The world is mine; I have found it.

You are lost in the sheer elation of having found your future. Con-
gratulations. But think of all you've found this way. Imagine some farmer
on a nameless day of backbreaking effort. He stumbles through a ground
too dry. His oxen use their brambled tails to swat at flies. The merciless sun
draws the sticky sweat from every pore of his body. Salty perspiration runs
into the corners of his eyes, stinging them with fire. Round and round the
fields he plows. His earth-stained hands now wrap the cracked reins around
the split wood handles of his plow. He stumbles again and again down
endless furrows. He turns the dry earth even as it furnishes him a shallow
ditch in which to walk.
Then in the middle of this staggering humdrum, the old plowshare
strikes something hard. Dry, hot sparks jump like flint from the earth. The
plow stops. The oxen will not budge. He must remove the flinty rock that
has hung the plow. But as he goes to remove the rock, he can see it is not a
rock. It is an iron box. He pries it from the earth. He beats its rusty hinges
till they split away. The box is open!
There greets him a huge, fiery, glittering treasure of gold and silver and
precious gems. He looks all about to be sure none have seen him make his

discovery. He quickly burrows back into the earth and hides the treasure where he found it. He is all through plowing for the day. He puts the oxen in the barn. He barely takes time to clean the field grime from his sweaty body.

He holds a delirious secret. He has found it.

Let the humdrum be damned forever!

There is a treasure in his field!

Only it is not his field—it belongs to another! He is only the share-cropper. He hurries to the registry and takes the last of his world's goods and buys the field.

Now is he truly rich.

"Mine, mine, mine!" he cries.

Remember the humdrum in which you lived? Remember how I came to you with great treasure? Remember your excitement? Remember how you cried, "Mine, mine, mine"? You had been refreshed by grace. Your endless plowing in the infertile furrows of your life had at last yielded treasure. You found it. All is well, forever!

LORD JESUS,
when first I found you,
elation was my unforsaking companion.
The treasure from the field
was buried in my heart of hearts.

The joy I'd come to own at last owned me.
Praise swelled the anthem of my liberty.
Amen.

114

Rebuking the Winds
of Fear

MARK 4:37-41

And there arose a fierce gale of wind, and the waves were breaking over the boat so much that the boat was already filling up. And
He Himself was in the stern, asleep on the cushion; and they awoke
Him and said to Him, "Teacher, do You not care that we are perishing?" And being aroused, He rebuked the wind and said to the sea,
"Hush, be still." And the wind died down and it became perfectly
calm. And He said to them, "Why are you so timid? How is it that
you have no faith?" And they became very much afraid and said
to one another, "Who then is this, that even the wind and the sea
obey Him?"

LORD,
I am stalked by fear. Things terrify me. They raise the
hair on the nape of my neck. I know you are master of
the monsters that hurry after me when the gloom is
thick and the night is dark. Help me. I'm afraid. Afraid
of the future. Afraid of the past. Afraid of all the shocks
that flesh is heir to.

I am unafraid. Let me still the fear that frightens you.
Awakened on the high seas, I once stared into the dark waves and roaring winds. Then I looked into the faces of my disciples. They were terrified. Fear is common in the human predicament, but fear in my presence
is inappropriate. One of those who grew so fearful in the face of the
encroaching storm was John, the apostle who would later write, "Perfect
love casts out fear" (1 John 4:18). He learned this great truth that night on
furious Galilee. Notice he did not say courage casts out fear; only love does
that.

Once fear owns your mind, courage is almost impossible to pluck up.
But love can serve you every time. A child may lay in the dark and tremble

before the unreal predators of darkness. But let her father walk in the room, and the child is suddenly made bold because in the presence of love, fear is driven out.

What of all the stories in which thin, frail women lift giant boulders or heavy fallen beams off their children in wild extraordinary circumstances? In better, ordinary days, such small mothers could in no way perform such Herculean feats. Remember, where passion is motivated by love, the strength is there to cast out fear.

For all those troubled apostles on Galilee that night, I ordered the storm away from the sea. It seemed no miracle to me; I had made the sea and the waves. They were mine. They had to obey me.

But the real miracle was that I calmed the inner storms of their frightened souls. With maturity these disciples would learn that no heart is large enough to contain both terror and my presence. You too must learn this. When I inhabit your heart, your fear must move aside to make a place for peace. The storms upon the wild and outer seas of your life cannot threaten you. Let me live fully in your heart. The storms are then barred from your life. The only fear you then will have to conquer lies in the weather of your heart.

LORD JESUS,
why do I always run
before the storms?
Why do I not remember my
heavenly Father's love
and rebuke my fears?
I beg you,
make safe my trembling heart.

In terrifying arctics keep me warm;
teach me the art of sleeping through a storm.
Amen.

115

LEGION: THE MANY FACES OF FEAR

LUKE 8:26-30

And they sailed to the country of the Gerasenes, which is opposite Galilee. And when He had come out onto the land, He was met by a certain man from the city who was possessed with demons; and who had not put on any clothing for a long time, and was not living in a house, but in the tombs. And seeing Jesus, he cried out and fell before Him, and said in a loud voice, "What did I have to do with You, Jesus, Son of the Most High God? I beg You, do not torment me." For He had been commanding the unclean spirit to come out of the man. For it had seized him many times; and he was bound with chains and shackles and kept under guard; and yet he would burst his fetters and be driven by the demon into the desert. And Jesus asked him, "What is your name?" And he said, "Legion"; for many demons had entered him.

LORD,
I am a composite of voices. Part of me wants to be dedicated. Part of me craves hedonism. Part of me wants to serve, part of me wants others to serve me. I want indulgence and self-sacrifice at the same time. Conflict fills me. I am torn by craving the illicit and the chaste at the same time.

When I came to the region of Gerasa, I met a man owned by his inner conflicts. He was an unkempt giant who frightened both children and adults. In his fierce rage he had broken chains.

My Father is called the Creator. Satan is often called *Abaddon* in the Hebrew and *Apollyon* in the Greek. Both of these words simply mean "the Destroyer." A creator finds great joy in making things. A destroyer only finds his great joy in destroying them.

Creativity calls for rest and assessment. Destroying things never needs to stop and rest. Destructive lust knows only that drivenness that must hurry on, ever destroying. The destroyer can never be happy until chaos and utter destruction owns the day. The destroyer never smiles out of pleasure; he only weeps with sadness when there is no more beauty left to dismantle.

Are you like Legion? Did God make you whole and clean and sovereign over all of life? But now you must reckon with the destroyer. He wants to destroy every value you possess. If he has his way, you will end up broken, mentally splintered, and possessed of dark forces. He longs to rave in the unholy caverns of your mind. Terror is Satan's chisel; it splits your confidence apart.

So when I saw Legion, he seemed an overpowering monster. But I saw what others could not. I saw this huge man not as an ugly threatening ogre but a child terrified of the hellish conflicts inside him.

I want to heal you too. I want to take your irrational fears and cast them out. I want to take your financial and occupational fears and cast them out. Your family fears, your health fears, you future fears—I want them all. Is your name Legion? If so, stand still, and I will cast out all that makes you seem complex when in actuality you are only afraid.

LORD JESUS,
I see you and submit.
The enemy is seeking to destroy
every beautiful value of my life.

I shall know peace, and then shall all be well.
Cast out my fears—these ugly dogs of hell.
Amen.

116

PORK THERAPY

LUKE 8:32-35

Now there was a herd of many swine feeding there on the mountain; and the demons entreated Him to permit them to enter the swine. And He gave them permission. And the demons came out from the man and entered the swine; and the herd rushed down the steep bank into the lake, and were drowned. And when the herdsmen saw what had happened, they ran away and reported it in the city and out in the country. And the people went out to see what had happened; and they came to Jesus, and found the man from whom the demons had gone out, sitting down at the feet of Jesus, clothed and in his right mind; and they became frightened.

LORD,
the greatest liberty I have ever imagined is just to know I am free. It feels so good to wake up in the morning knowing I belong to a gracious God who will not let me die as the victim of my rash uncertainties. I love you.

The demons that circled you and barred your trek into the destiny my Father planned for you have been ordered into the abyss. The future is yours. Rejoice! That's what God is all about—the future!

The demons on the day of Legion's healing begged to be sent into a herd of pigs. Why pigs? Because demons are a homeless lot. In their homelessness they fear having to return to the abyss. So I responded to their request. Why was I so nice to these grungy little nomads—these destroyers of a poor man's peace? I did not befriend the demons so much as I gave the demoniac a visible evidence that they were gone. Legion beheld the pigs rush over the precipice and perish in the sea. Their wild behavior was a powerful evidence to him that he had been healed.

No illness can be cured absolutely without some pronouncement that it is over. Until the physician says, "You have a clean bill of health," the mere hope of health is too fleeting to offer us much peace. The crazed pigs were my final way of saying to Legion, "Your ordeal is over. The demons, as you have just seen, have perished."

Consider two patients cured of an incurable disease. In the one case the doctor says, "You are free of this disease forever." In the other case the doctor says, "You are free of this disease forever, I think." The lack of certitude in the second patient is a cancer all its own—a cancer of anxiety that eats at peace. In the end, not knowing may be worse than the disease itself.

Peace for you is not merely having your demons exorcised. Peace is *knowing* your demons are gone. Watching them perish forever, the cleansed know they are truly clean. Trust what you know of grace. You have seen Calvary. Know for sure you are healed.

LORD JESUS,
the certainty of healing
is your greatest gift.
Such security is forever.

In watching every plaguing devil go,
I praise you that I know, I know, I know.
Amen.

117

THE NON-EXOTIC ASSIGNMENT

MARK 5:18-20

And as He was getting into the boat, the man who had been demon-possessed was entreating Him that he might accompany Him. And He did not let him, but He said to him, "Go home to your people and report to them what great things the Lord has done for you, and how He had mercy on you." And he went away and began to proclaim in Decapolis what great things Jesus had done for him; and everyone marveled.

LORD,
I'm tired of serving you here at home. I want to go somewhere exotic. I want to serve you where there are distant cultures and lots of new things. But mostly there are people I don't know. The people I know are really hard to like. The problem is we know each other too well. Lord, send me to people I don't know. I want to try loving them for a while—new people always seem nicer than the people I know.

Legion felt like you feel. He wanted the excitement of going somewhere new for the same reasons you feel it.

"Go home!" I said to Legion. "There tell your countrymen what great things have happened to you." It was not what Legion wanted to hear. He wanted a more exotic assignment, a Christian adventure. He wanted something more executive and authoritative.

Why did he dread those words, "Go home and tell"? Because home is where they knew him well. Naturally he did not want to go back where everyone knew him. He wanted to go and make converts among those who didn't know him because there the baggage of his past would not be a problem.

I was shortly to go home to Nazareth, where my lofty claims were met by, "Isn't this the carpenter's kid?" Everyone owns less respect in the home country than elsewhere. Still, home has two great advantages. First, hometown folks will hear a family member before they will hear a stranger, however exotic. And second, a family member can get inside the inner sanctum of the familiar far faster than a stranger.

Genuine change is easier recognized by those inside the family than those outside.

If you doubt this, remember the impact my own family had on the world. My mother believed and obviously furnished some information to Luke for the writing of his Gospel. My brother James believed and became head of the church in Jerusalem. My brother Jude believed and became one of the writers of the New Testament. My faith was not widely accepted in Palestine, but it was deeply believed by my family, who surprised even themselves by becoming world changers.

My assignment to Legion is my assignment to you: I'm sending you home too. Go home, where the changes I have produced in your life will be everywhere evident. Go home to those who are skeptical of what you say you have become because they know what you used to be. Home is where your story must be told. If your faith will not stand at home, it will stand nowhere.

LORD JESUS,
I need to remember that
home is where it's easy to go
but where it's hard to be influential.

Does familiarity still breed contempt?
I'll serve you anyway—I'm not exempt.
Amen.

118

THE IMPORTANCE OF PUBLIC CONFESSION

LUKE 8:43-47

And a woman who had a hemorrhage for twelve years, and could not be healed by anyone, came up behind Him, and touched the fringe of His cloak; and immediately her hemorrhage stopped. And Jesus said, "Who is the one who touched Me?" And while they were all denying it, Peter said, "Master, the multitudes are crowding and pressing upon You." But Jesus said, "Someone did touch Me, for I was aware that power had gone out of Me." And when the woman saw that she had not escaped notice, she came trembling and fell down before Him, and declared in the presence of all the people the reason why she had touched Him, and how she had been immediately healed.

LORD,
I'm the quiet type, you know. You'll not find me showy or a braggart when it comes to grace. I live pretty much to myself. It's a favor I do for the world.

Remember this: Sometimes silence is golden, and sometimes it is cowardly. To receive the riches of grace and never mention it to a soul makes a clear statement about your value system. What we really live for, we cannot cease talking about.

I once met a very needy woman who took grace and kept the joy of it in silence. I felt her hand that day as one reaching out to me in need. She sought healing from the hem of my garment. In her reaching desperation, I felt my healing power flood out of me in vast amounts.

I stopped and said (not forcefully, for she was not far away), "Who touched me?" It seemed a foolish question in such a large crowd. Everybody had touched me. Still, the woman whose frail arm had struck out through the massive wall of people knew I meant her. She had been healed. She knew it instantly. I knew it too.

At my command the world around her stopped. I stopped. The crowd stopped. She came forward, timid and trembling, owning up to her healing. I rather forced her to acknowledge that she had been healed. It was not my intent to further brutalize her fragile spirit. Still, a huge principle was at stake for the kingdom. No one is ever free to receive great things from God and then slink back into the crowd without acknowledging the gift.

The kingdom I died to found has but one tactic of enlistment and growth: confession. Unless those who receive grace acknowledge what they have received, the kingdom cannot grow. The heart of the Christian faith is first, last, and always confession.

Are you prone to ask, "Well, do I have to confess Christ to be converted? Can I not be saved without this showy declaration?" Confession is your primary witness to the authenticity of my presence in your life. If a man and a woman marry in secret, their marriage is not lawful. Civil law declares that two witnesses must sign the marriage document. These witnesses must declare by signature that they heard and saw the couple make their life promises. No witnesses, no marriage!

Are you open about what I have given you? Have you acknowledged me before men that I may acknowledge you before my Father who is in heaven (Matthew 10:32)?

LORD JESUS,
I have received in private your salvation,
but I must bless you publicly for your gifts.

I met you in a darksome, lonely place
to publicly exalt your saving grace.
Amen.

119

CREDENTIALS

MARK 6:1-3

And He went out from there, and He came into His hometown; and His disciples followed Him. And when the Sabbath had come, He began to teach in the synagogue; and the many listeners were astonished, saying, "Where did this man get these things, and what is this wisdom given to Him, and such miracles as these performed by His hands? Is not this the carpenter, the son of Mary, and brother of James, and Joses, and Judas, and Simon? Are not His sisters here with us?" And they took offense at Him.

LORD,
I wish I had a PhD. Maybe then people would listen more to my opinions. Especially those people who knew me as a child. They say behind any successful person are the people who told him as a child that he'd never amount to anything.

I began my ministry by going to Nazareth to preach. I was God's Son, the Messiah. Those really are great credentials. This gladsome news fell fully on me at my baptism. I had gradually come to accept my genuine preexistence and virgin birth status as the Son of God after 40 days of wilderness struggles and desert temptations.

I was God's Son. But where would I go first to tell this gladsome news? Where would I go see my splendid credentials accepted? Why not home? Why not tell those wonderful hometown people the good news that God, Emmanuel, was in the world? Why not announce that I, their family, their kinsman and friend, was the Messiah?

So I stood in my own hometown to bring the news.

My family was there: Miriam, Joses, Judas. There was even another Joshua or two just like myself. How I loved them. In every face I saw a friend. I saw old women who had prayed for me through childhood sicknesses. I studied old, weathered patriarchs who had told me Bible stories in our little synagogue. I saw school chums who had memorized a thousand Scriptures with me while we prepared for our bar mitzvahs.

They were glad I had come home.

"Read for us!" they cried, "Yes, Jesus, read for us!"

I walked to the front of the synagogue. A leathery old Rabbi picked up the scroll of Isaiah and brought it to me. I unrolled it slowly while a hush fell over the little congregation. Then I stopped unrolling the scroll, and I read:

> The Spirit of the Lord is upon Me,
> Because He anointed Me to preach the gospel to the
>   poor.
> He has sent Me to proclaim release to the captives,
> And recovery of sight to the blind,
> To set free those who are downtrodden,
> To proclaim the favorable year of the Lord (Luke
>   4:18-19).

I sat down the scroll and said, "This day is this scripture fulfilled in your ears" (Luke 4:21 KJV).

But my hometown friends, who might have made Nazareth the cradle of Christianity, were skeptical. They fidgeted in doubt. They grew angry. They left the world's greatest truth to be decided by others who would trust me more because their hearts were not made small by harsh familiarity.

LORD JESUS,
*I want to have a ready response
in the face of every skeptic.
I want to proclaim you
in full belief and utter open courage.*

*You perfectly interpreted God's Word.
I now, in perfect faith, must call you Lord.
Amen.*

120

THE LIMITING LITTLENESS

MARK 6:4-6

And Jesus said to them, "A prophet is not without honor except in his home town and among his own relatives and in his own household." And He could do no miracle there except that He laid His hands upon a few sick people and healed them. And He wondered at their unbelief. And He was going around the villages teaching.

LORD,
my hometown is filled with people you love, but I don't care much for them—at least not for all of them. They are so tied to yesterday. Were there people like that in Nazareth? If so, you must have stayed away from home a lot.

No prophet in his own hometown is capable of honor. He cannot achieve great things there. The unbelief of those who know the prophet will keep great things from happening. Now consider the cost of my rejection in Nazareth: I could do for them no mighty work because of their unbelief.

Consider the cost of unbelief: Kingdoms fall. The sick die needlessly. The brokenhearted commit suicide. Orphans grieve. Widows live disconsolately. Faith, like a grain of mustard seed, can move mountains. Yet hometown skeptics stand in the way of miracles. No mustard seed can grow in Nazareth.

However, before you are too severe on these Nazarenes, consider the price of unbelief in your life. Do you not see how even the most ordinary crisis evokes the same response in you? Crisis comes, and instead of meeting it with faith, you crumble in your fear. You check your bank account to see if you can handle things financially. Then you tell your poor, weak, human friends of the severity of your crisis.

"Poor thing—we pity you!" they say. Their pity is worthless, yet you treasure it.

Alas, when you have tried every other avenue, it suddenly occurs to you that you are a Christian. Then finally you turn to me for help. Going last where you should have gone first, you find me all sufficient. Then you believe. Gratefully, at long last you trust. I destroy the crisis. How costly is unbelief?

So it was in Nazareth. They wanted me to do at home what I had done elsewhere. But at home they tied my hands with skepticism before they begged me to demonstrate my power. I had no choice but to go to proclaim my full messiahship elsewhere—to those whose hearts were larger.

Come to me. I am able to meet your every need. Give me your trust and then stand back.

LORD JESUS,
so much I might
have meant to you is past.
I cannot scrape it back together for a second pass.
I held you at arm's length, knowing that

God's deeds are snatched by one foul, petty thief—
a bandit known to God as unbelief.
Amen.

121

VENTURING INTO MY SUFFICIENCY

LUKE 9:1-3
And He called the twelve together, and gave them power and authority over all the demons, and to heal diseases. And He sent them out to proclaim the kingdom of God, and to perform healing. And He said to them, "Take nothing for your journey, neither a staff, nor a bag, nor bread, nor money, and do not even have two tunics apiece."

LORD,
I long to need you. I want to feel your Spirit creating my world anew. I want to turn from my independence to utter dependence on you. Perhaps then I'll experience the mystery that comes from total reliance on the work of the Spirit.

I once sent the 12 out on a preaching tour with no supplies. I gave them no money or extra clothing to carry with them. I wanted them to learn what I already knew: To have the means to do my work without needing me almost always leads to doing it without me.

You too may need to remember that self-reliance can be a pit in the path of your dependency.

To have sufficient means to accomplish something great in my name often ends in feelings of pride for having achieved the thing on your own. Self-reliance is easily subverted into self-seeking. The best way to avoid self-seeking in life is to surrender your need to acquire those material things that will in time lead you to become self-reliant. This is why I asked my disciples not to take anything with them on the preaching tour—not a cane, not money, not even an extra tunic.

When Francis of Assisi began to take the kingdom of God to the poor and the mentally ill, he dressed only in hair-cloth and begged his bread from door to door. In begging his bread, he remained dependent on such simple fare as begging provided. Begging is not an occupation one brags about. So there grew up around his begging an institution of mercy that could not be credited to his own clever financial achievements. Only when God is all you have will he get the credit for all you accomplish.

How often has a small church preached and achieved some glorious dream? When they began that dream, they were pure of heart and willing that God should have all the credit. But once they succeeded, they found they had to adopt an operating budget. Next they hired a large staff. Then came affluence and pulpit memorials. Little brass donation plaques rose beside pulpits and organ pipes. The great stained-glass windows contained leaded panels with the names of those generous Christians who had made the splendor possible.

Everything that happens in some churches is fully explainable in terms of human resources. But here and there some churches exist who have not forgotten their call to servanthood. These still gird their waists with towels and carry the basin of ministry into the world they are called to serve. They have no money, no power members, no famous preachers. They walk in their world simply—no staff, no bag, no bread, no money. They depend on me and me alone. They are a Pentecost in embryo. Their only ensigns are fire and wind.

LORD JESUS,
we have planned too well for success.
We have read every manual on the subject.
We have stored up the necessary finances.
We have secured the pledges,
and we have the signatures of the significant
all filed away on faith-promise cards.

But we shall fail without a Christ desire,
achieving nothing without wind and fire.
Amen.

122

THE DOUBLE OBLIGATION

MATTHEW 10:14-16

And whoever does not receive you, nor heed your words, as you go out of that house or that city, shake off the dust of your feet. Truly I say to you, it will be more tolerable for the land of Sodom and Gomorrah in the day of judgment, than for that city. Behold, I send you out as sheep in the midst of wolves; therefore be shrewd as serpents, and innocent as doves.

LORD,
I know I have the obligation to speak on your behalf, but is anybody obligated to listen? Serving you is the only point in living, but I want to know this: When I have taken my strongest stand, is anyone out there obligated to pay attention?

Never forget the bottom line as you minister: You are not accountable for your success or failure in any human arena. Nothing I have called you to do in my name in this world will be dismissed as trivial in that world to which you are headed. If you are rejected in your attempt to preach the truth, the truth that caused your rejection will not be judged by those who turn a deaf ear to your counsel. Those who reject your words must themselves face the last tribunal.

So never despair over rejection. I knew rejection firsthand. I never despaired. The greatest truths are regularly rejected. You do not need to win any battle in the same moment you take up arms. As I told my disciples as they began their preaching tour, if you are cast out of any city, do not try to barge back into it to compel anyone to listen. Just shake the dust off your feet. Why? Because those who hear the truth need to remember that the truth of the gospel is not an option left up to human caprice. The shaking of the dust from your feet will remind those who listen of their obligation to hear.

The gospel has always carried this double obligation. It obligates the disciple to tell the message and the seeker to listen. Pity the complacent witness who will not tell the saving story. Pity the complacent seeker who will not hear it.

But in this double obligation, important as it is, you must never merely count your converts to measure your success. Truth is its own reward. Once you have told the truth, you have succeeded. Telling the saving truth is your responsibility. Doing the saving is mine. Counting converts is unnecessary. It is an unworthy bottom line on earth and unessential in heaven. So do not grow neurotic trying to become a savior yourself. That is my title; I will do that work. That should take quite a load off your mind. You are only responsible for telling the truth. So tell it. If thousands are drawn to the faith, you will succeed. If you die without a single convert and are crucified for telling the truth, you will still have succeeded.

Still, tact is the lubricant of acceptance. Tact does not mean you flatter people so they will like you. "Shrewd as serpents, harmless as doves"—this is the rule. Be shrewd like the snake, whose lowly existence requires him to keep out from under people's boots. Snakes know the principles of their own survival: Keep to the side of the path; avoid the crush of commerce. But also be like a dove. These gentle creatures make no one afraid. Their softness invites all to know them.

LORD JESUS,
I need to learn to travel
through my world negotiating the hostile traffic
and the crowds of skeptics.
Help me to learn the difference between tact and cowardice.
Help me accept my obligation to tell the truth
and to understand the obligation of my listeners to hear it.

Responsibility is best served it seems,
when I but preach the truth, and you redeem.
Amen.

123

THE INNER VOICE

MATTHEW 10:17-20

But beware of men: for they will deliver you up to the courts, and scourge you in their synagogues; and you shall even be brought before governors and kings for My sake, as a testimony to them and to the Gentiles. But when they deliver you up, do not become anxious about how or what you will speak; for it shall be given you in that hour what you are to speak. For it is not you who speak, but it is the Spirit of your Father who speaks in you.

LORD, you sometimes seem to require so much more of me than I can ever accomplish. You put me into situations that appear too grand for me. I feel very uncomfortable. I'm an ordinary person. Please don't push me into arenas where I am terrified. Sophistication scares me. What am I to do?

Your intimidation by life is more customary than you think. Nothing really great can be achieved till you are willing to leave your comfort zone. Only when your circumstances get edgy will you strike out for the perilous ledges of real advancement.

My presence within you was never intended to lie inoperative. There are those who want God's Holy Spirit to sleep within them like a pink coma.

My inner presence is neither sweet nor sleepy. I am a raging fire. I am a restless cry within your breast. I am not a passive indweller. I am the Roar of Life, the Morning Thunder, the Lightning of life eternal. To permit me in your life is to dissolve your ego in the acid of my power. All of this is to help you become what you were born to be. So if you have to make your bed in hell, do it in confidence. Pity all who judge you, for anyone who judges you must later reckon with heaven.

Do you wish to make demons flee at your command? Then greet them with that power—God's power, not your own—that resides in your heart. Set the roaring God free within you. Let him force these threatening serpents back into the abyss. God will cap them in steel and bury them forever in the deepest part of hell, from where they came. All of this will be at your command.

What makes you afraid?

I told my disciples of the fear they would feel when they came before human tribunals and were forced to answer. I reminded them that in their hour of need they would meet my sufficiency. The same principle holds true for you. You have the same wonderful indwelling Spirit they had. Being afraid is human, but to be paralyzed by your fear while I indwell your life is a denial of my power. It is ungodly to be a Christian and live a weak life, napping through the years in your comfort zone.

Fear no longer.

Open your heart. The Enemy will see and flee before the formidable power within you.

LORD JESUS,
help me remember that when I trusted you,
you filled my life
with such force
that I knew I would never again face a single threat
you could not successfully handle.

And here I am, my heart of Spirit-steel is made.
Be gone, poor hell! For heaven's unafraid!
Amen.

Other Good ———— Harvest House Reading

God's Best for My Life
Dr. Lloyd John Ogilvie

We all need fresh grace each day, says Dr. Lloyd John Ogilvie in his bestselling *God's Best for My Life* (more than 146,000 copies sold). Now available in a smaller, more convenient size, this handy daily devotional by the former chaplain of the United States Senate offers 365 days of insight, encouragement, and hope.

Quiet Moments with God
Lloyd John Ogilvie

These daily, heartfelt prayers will help you nurture a special intimacy with God. You will truly experience God's blessed assurance as you are comforted by His boundless love and promises to provide guidance and give strength.

Daily in Christ
Neil and Joanne Anderson

Tired of trying to live the Christian life in your own strength? This 365-day devotional is a refreshing invitation to live *in Christ* and be refreshed by the Father's love.

HARVEST HOUSE
PUBLISHERS